1 MONTH OF
FREE
READING

at
www.ForgottenBooks.com

By purchasing this book you are eligible for one month membership to ForgottenBooks.com, giving you unlimited access to our entire collection of over 1,000,000 titles via our web site and mobile apps.

To claim your free month visit:
www.forgottenbooks.com/free902067

ISBN 978-0-265-86927-7
PIBN 10902067

UNITED STATES DEPARTMENT OF AGRICULTURE
SOIL CONSERVATION SERVICE - RESEARCH
WASHINGTON, D. C.

In cooperation with
Maryland, Delaware, and New Jersey
Agricultural Experiment Stations

RATES OF RUNOFF
IN THE
COASTAL PLAINS OF NEW JERSEY, DELAWARE, AND MARYLAND

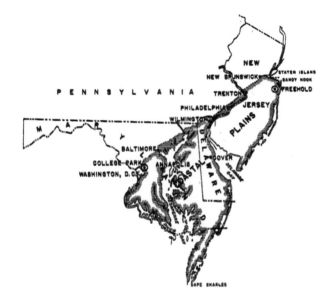

By Harold W. Hobbs, Agricultural Engineer
Division of Drainage and Water Control

Under the Technical Direction of
D. B. Krimgold, Soil Conservationist

3
SCS-TP-60
July 1946

FOREWORD

This publication is one of a series of reports containing information for the hydrologic design of conservation structures and practices on agricultural lands in basic land-resource areas in the United States. The information, procedures, and recommendations contained in these reports are based on runoff, rainfall, and other hydrologic data obtained in runoff research and other research projects conducted by the Soil Conservation Service in cooperation with the State agricultural experiment stations. United States Weather Bureau records of precipitation and other data, records of stream flow of the United States Geological Survey, and available records from other sources are used in these publications.

This report is limited to peak rates of runoff for design purposes and constitutes the first two parts of a publication which will cover, in addition to peak rates, a third part on the total runoff yields in relation to their distribution and frequency of recurrence. Information on peak rates is being released at this time to meet the urgent need for this type of data.

Basic hydrologic data for the Coastal Plains, particularly runoff records from small agricultural watersheds, are still very limited with respect to range in watershed size, length of record, soil conditions represented, and land-use practices investigated. There is a lack of adequate information on the inter-relation of rates and amounts of runoff to size of drainage area under pasture, plowland, and woodland use, for various soil-condition complexes. Runoff investigations must be conducted over a sufficient period of years to verify the values of the frequency of recurrence of 10- and 25-year rates used in this report. Accordingly, the information presented herein is considered as tentative and subject to revision when more reliable data from longer periods of record have been collected and additional studies undertaken to make up the deficiencies in basic hydrologic data.

Tables 4, 5, 6, 7, and 8 and figures 2, 3, 4, and 5 of this publication, together with pertinent instructions and recommendations, have been prepared in such form that they can be used in handbooks or instructions of agencies concerned with the planning and financing of conservation and drainage structures in the Coastal Plains area in New Jersey, Maryland, and Delaware.

M. L. Nichols
Chief of Research

ACKNOWLEDGMENTS

The establishment of the runoff and agricultural hydrologic studies and the collection of records which form the basis of this report involved the work of the author and other members of the Division of Drainage and Water Control, Soil Conservation Service-- Research, as well as Operations' personnel and members of the New Jersey and Maryland Agricultural Experiment Station staffs. The runoff studies at Freehold, N. J., were carried out under a memorandum of understanding between the Soil Conservation Service and the New Jersey Agricultural Experiment Station in accordance with approved working plans. The agricultural hydrologic studies at College Park, Md., were carried out jointly under the cooperative project agreement and working plans between the University of Maryland Agricultural Experiment Station and the Soil Conservation Service, United States Department of Agriculture.

Messrs. G. W. Eley, A. T. Roth, G. W. Grisdale, Jr., and J. J. Pellett, members of Operations' technical staff at Freehold, deserve outstanding recognition for the competent handling of construction and maintenance of the installations and of the collection of records.

The ready cooperation of the members of the Maryland Experiment Station staff in the construction of the College Park installations, in carrying out the cropping operations, and in aiding the studies in many other ways is greatly appreciated.

In delineating the general area of application (map on cover page) and the specific soil and agricultural conditions within this area to which the data apply, the author is greatly indebted to Dr. W. J. Latimer and W. ˮ Hearn of the Bureau of Plant Industry, Soils, and Agricultural Engineering; Messrs. M. F. Hershberger, A. M. O'Neal, K. P. Wilson, R. K. Craver, and O. R. Neal, Soil Conservation Service; and Dr. R. P. Thomas of the Maryland Agricultural Experiment Station.

The comments and suggestions of Drs. W. B. Kemp, William Martin, and G. L. Schuster, directors of the Agricultural Experiment Stations in Maryland, New Jersey, and Delaware, respectively, together with those of Dr. Austin L. Patrick, regional conservator, Northeast region, Soil Conservation Service, and C. S. Slater, project supervisor of the Soil Conservation Laboratory, College Park, Md., all of whom reviewed the original draft, are much appreciated.

The author is especially indebted to D. B. Krimgold, soil conservationist, under whose technical direction the report was prepared, for suggestions on procedures and many of the techniques for analyses of the data, together with direct collaboration in carrying them out. The comments and information given by C. E. Ramser, research specialist in hydrology, are acknowledged with gratitude. The suggestions of W. D. Potter, hydraulic engineer, for the arrangement of the final publication are greatly appreciated.

The assistance of Freeman W. Snyder, agricultural engineer, in collecting and compiling the basic data, making routine analyses, and assembling the report is gratefully acknowledged, together with the painstaking help of Miss Georgie A. Keller in editing and assembling the final draft. The studies near Freehold, N. J., were made possibly by the interest and cooperation of the owners and operators of the land involved.

RATES OF RUNOFF
IN THE
COASTAL PLAINS OF NEW JERSEY, DELAWARE, AND MARYLAND

CONTENTS

Tables

Plates

RATES OF RUNOFF
IN THE
COASTAL PLAINS OF NEW JERSEY, DELAWARE, AND MARYLAND

by

Harold W. Hobbs, Agricultural Engineer

INTRODUCTION

The need for information on the peak rates and amounts of runoff from small agricultural drainage areas has long been recognized by agricultural workers and engineers.
The early lay-out and increasing use of roads and highways, and later, railroads, com-
pelled the gradual improvement of their drainage facilities. The choice of size of openings for culverts and bridges to handle runoff from agricultural areas had to be made.
This was done by guesswork at first and later by empirical formulas based largely on
rationalization from runoff data from larger drainages. When culverts or bridges washed
out from flood peaks, the openings were generally enlarged when they were rebuilt. Such
cut and try methods of design were costly.

The first actual runoff information for small areas came from Ramser's exploratory
studies in 1917 and 1918 on the 6 field-size areas ranging from 1.25 to 112 acres on the
Murchison farm near Jackson, Tenn.[1] In 1933, when the extensive program of soil conservation got under way, Ramser published a set of curves[2] for unterraced areas. These were
based largely on the Jackson results and data obtained on small watersheds located on
several of the first 10 Federal soil erosion experiment stations established in 1929.
The curves gave recommended runoff rates in cubic feet per second for drainage areas of
1 to 1,000 acres for 'rolling' timber, pasture, and cultivated areas, and higher rates
for 'hilly' conditions. These curves applied directly to the area included in Meyer's
Group 3 of States extending from Kansas to Massachusetts.[3] Factors were supplied for
Meyer's four other groups of States lying east of the Rocky Mountains, by which the
Group 3 curve values could be reduced for the more northerly locations, and increased
for the areas to the south. These curves were widely used, not only in the regions
recommended by Ramser, but also in the Western States. Early in 1935, runoff curves for
terraced areas[4] were also distributed to agricultural workers, giving Ramser's recommendations. With the publication late in 1935 of Yarnell's bulletin on rainfall intensity-frequency data[5] the use of Ramser's runoff coefficients in the rational method
was extended to all parts of the United States.

---

[1]RAMSER, C. E. RUNOFF FROM SMALL AGRICULTURAL AREAS. Jour. of Agr. Res. 34: 797-
823, illus. 1927.

[2]RAMSER, C. E. BRIEF INSTRUCTIONS ON METHODS OF GULLY CONTROL. U. S. Dept. Agr., Bur.
Agr. Engin. 35 pp., illus. 1933. [Mimeographed.]

[3]MEYER, A. F. ELEMENTS OF HYDROLOGY. p. 166, Ed. 2. John Wiley and Sons, New York.
1928.

[4]ELLISON, W. D. ENGINEERING PRACTICES AND STANDARD PLANS FOR E. C. W. EROSION CONTROL
CAMPS. U. S. Soil Conserv. Tech. Pub. 12. 69 pp., illus. 1936. [Mimeographed.]

[5]YARNELL, D. L. RAINFALL INTENSITY-FREQUENCY DATA. U. S. Dept. Agr. Misc. Pub. 204,
67 pp., illus. 1935.

However, general observations by workers in various oarts of the country, together
with preliminary results from the erosion experiment stations, indicated the inadvisa-
bility of applying the limited data from Tennessee and elsewhere in such a widespread
manner. The available rainfall-intensity data proved inadequate as a tool for applying
the meager runoff information to remote areas. It soon became evident that rainfall intensity and amount were only two of a number of factors which determine the intensity of
runoff from a given area at a particular time.

Recognizing the urgent necessity for obtaining runoff rates and amounts more nearly
applicable to the various regions of the country, plans were developed late in 1936 by the
Soil Conservation Service for initiating runoff studies on farms in demonstration projects.
Later, similar studies were inaugurated on State-owned lands administered by State agri-
cultural experiment stations. *(See fig. 1.)* As a part of the Nation-wide program of this
phase of soil conservation research, four watersheds were selected on farms near Freehold,
N. J., as representing conditions typical of the northern Coastal Plains area of New
Jersey, Delaware, and Maryland. For administrative reasons, the selection of the Freehold watersheds had to be restricted to willing cooperators of the 17,133-acre Manalapan
Creek Demonstration Project. Runoff and precipitation stations were constructed on the
watersheds in 1937, and the collection of records began in February 1938. These stations
were discontinued in October 1943 with almost 6 years of runoff data available.

In 1939, in cooperation with the University of Maryland Agricultural Experiment Station, the Soil Conservation Service set up agricultural hydrologic studies on the Plant
Research farm of the station, which is located northwest of College Park, Md. The choice
of areas in this case was even more restricted as the only available land consisted of the
528-acre farm. The areas selected, therefore, do not represent every condition in the
Coastal Plains area. It is felt, however, that the experimental watersheds are typical
of a good deal of the agricultural land in this land-resource area. Five watersheds were
put into operation in 1939, and four additional drainage areas in 1940. In 1943, a tenth
experimental watershed was added. The College Park studies are still being carried on and
at the time of this report have furnished 3 to 6 years of runoff records from which to
estimate the probable frequencies of recurrence of peak rates of flow, under various agricultural practices.

PART I

GENERAL DESCRIPTION OF THE EXPERIMENTAL WATERSHEDS

The characteristics of the Freehold and College Park watersheds are summarized in
tables 1 and 2. They are more fully described under the heading 'Detailed Descriptions of
the Experimental Areas' in Part II of this report.

The term 'prevailing slope' refers to slopes occupying 30 percent or more of the
area. The length of the principal waterway is the distance in feet from the gaging station along the drainageway to the point where water concentrates sufficiently to produce
channel flow. The slope of the principal waterway is the average slope from beginning to
end of its length. The drainage density is the total length of all waterways in feet divided by the area in acres. The form factor is a dimensionless number serving as an index of the shape of the watershed. The area in square feet is divided by the square of
the length of the watershed measured in a straight line in the general direction of the
principal waterway. In cases of watersheds lying all to one side of the principal drainageway, a single diversion terrace for example, the area is doubled and shown over a
denominator of 2. On cropland-terraced areas the index probably has no significance.

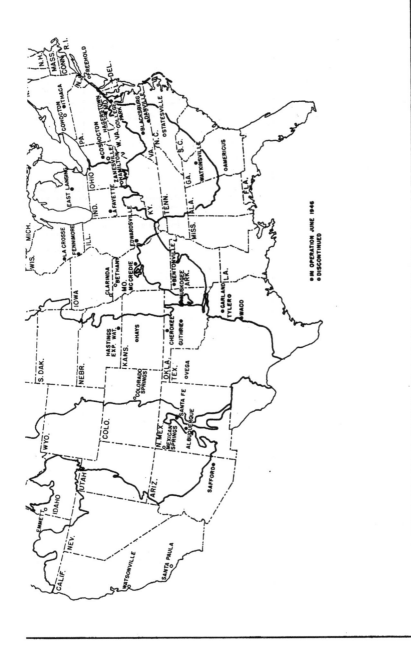

Figure I. Runoff and Experimental Watershed studies conducted in the Major Land Resource areas by the Soil Conservation Service

TABLE I.--*Characteristics of the Freehold, N. J., drainage areas*

Watershed designation	H. Surgent (W-I)	T. Smith (W-II)	J. Sherrard (W-III)	W. Ward (W-IV)
Area - acres	15.7 to Aug. '38, increased to 17.5.	34.2 to Feb. '39, reduced to 32.9	51.8	102.7
Length watershed - feet	1,210	1,860	2,910	3,550
Average width - feet	630	770	775	1,260
Soils: Physical characteristics	Light textured, deep, well-drained.	Light textured, deep, well-drained.	Light textured, deep to moderately deep, well-drained.	Light textured, de well to excessivel drained.[1]
Major type or types	Freehold sandy loam.	Freehold sandy loam..	Freehold sandy loam and loam.	Freehold sandy loe loamy sand.
Range in depth - inches	18 to 38	18 to 82	8 to 36	18 to 36
Average depth or average depth to impeding stratum - inches	35	42	32	35
Range in land slope - percent	1 to 12	1 to 15	0.8 to 15	1 to 12
Prevailing land slope or slopes - percent	3	2.5 and 5	1.5 and 5	2 and 5
Length of principal waterway - feet	945	1,340	2,350	2,050
Average slope of principal waterway - percent	2.86	2.82	1.53	1.70
Drainage density - length of waterways per acre - feet per acre	363	144	70.1	52.1
Form factor $\frac{A}{L^2}$ A = area in square feet L = length of area in feet	0.976	0.428	0.310	0.580
Land Use	Cropland terraces, planted to truck crops on contour.	Potatoes and general crops planted off-contour, 17% strip cropped.	Potatoes and general crops planted off-contour, 22% pasture.	Potatoes and gene planted off-contor

[1]Freehold loamy sand occupies only 17 percent of area, 6 percent in drainageways.

Watershed designation	W-I (paired with W-II)	W-II (paired with W-I)	W-III (paired with W-IV)	W-IV (paired with W-III)	W-V (paired with W-X)	W-VI (paired with W-VII)	W-VII (paired with W-VI)	W-VIII	W-IX	W-X (paired with W-V)
Area - acres	8.22	7.44	5.66 to Apr.'44; increased to 6.06, May '44; reduced to 5.05, Sept. '44.	8.01 to Apr.'44; reduced to 6.11, May '44; and to 5.05, Sept. '44.	4.07	3.53	4.10, reduced to 3.52 in Aug. 1941.	2.45	12.05	3.04
Length watershed-feet / Average width-feet	1,100 / 305	1,130 / 287	900[1] / 293[1]	880[2] / 302[2]	1,040 / 170	710 / 217	750[3] / 204[3]	540 / 195	1,300 / 404	615 / 215
Soils: Physical characteristics	Medium textured, moderately deep, imperf. drained.	Light text., deep, to mod. deep, well-drained.	Light textured, deep, well-drained.	Light text., deep, well to imperf. drained.	Light textured, moderately deep, well-drained.	Med. to light text., mod. deep, well to imperf. drained.	Medium textured, shallow, imperf. drained.	Medium textured, shallow, imperf. drained.	Light textured, med. deep, well-drained.	Light to med. text., shallow to mod. deep, well to imperf. drained.
Major type or types	Beltsville and Leonardtown loams.	Chilum gravelly loam and loam, Hyattsville loam.	Sassafras loam and sandy loam.	Beltsville and Sassafras loams.	Chilum loam & gravelly loams.	Chilum sandy loam & Beltsv. silt loam.	Beltsville silt loam.	Beltsville silt loam.	Chilum loam, gravelly loam, & sandy loam.	Chilum grav. loam, Beltsv. silt loam, Croom grav. loam.
Range in depth - inches	14 to 43	8 to 48	36 to 48	36 to 48	9 to 48	9 to 48	5 to 48	18 to 36	13 to 48	6 to 48
Average depth or average depth to impeding stratum - inches	27	34	47	46	26	26	18	23	22	20
Range in land slope - percent	1 to 10	2 to 17	1 to 10	1 to 12	3 to 15	3 to 11	3 to 15	3 to 15	2 to 17	3 to 15
Prevailing land slope or slopes - percent	5 and 7	4 and 10	4 and 6	4 and 8	4 and 9	6	4 and 9	6	4 and 9	4 and 10
Length of principal waterway - feet	1,400	1,100	1,150	870	1,000	730	600	220	1,040	680
Slope of principal waterway - percent	5.0	5.1	1.5	2.0	0.44	4.0	4.0	6.4	3.6	0.90
Drainage density - length of waterways per acre - feet per acre	207	215	401	245	245	400	935	123	105	197
Form factor $\frac{A}{L^2}$; A = area in square feet; L = Length of area in feet	0.296	0.254	0.326	0.344	0.354/2	0.328	0.367	0.363	0.311	0.700/2
Land use	Both, strip-cropped within 2% of contour; 96 ft. uniform strips. Rotation corn, grain, and hay. (Aug. 1939 to Oct. 1943.) Same rotation in strip cropping 1942 to 1945.	Up & down in tillage (Nov. '42 to '45).	Both in pasture Oct.'39-Apr.'41. Soybeans & rye drilled up & down May '41 to Apr. '42. Truck crops '42-'44.	Contour '42, & down in '43 & '44, contour after Sept. '44.	Contour tillage above diversion terrace in 3 fields, but not strip-cropped. 3-yr. rotation corn (or sorg.)- grain & hay'sorg. '39 to Oct.'43.	Both areas, pastures under common treatment, heavily grazed '40 to Apr. 1943. Pasture continued May '43 to '46.	20 ft. pasture, furrows from May '43. Manure fertilized and seeded 1944.	Ungrazed cut-over woodland: shrubs, hardwoods and scrub pine. Good to poor litter with occasional bare spots. Burned over in past.	Mature woodland: mixed hardwoods and scrub pine. Ungrazed and unburned. Excellent litter.	Mature woodland-strip cropping on mixed hardwoods exact contour above diversion terrace, and scrub pine. Ungrazed and unburned. Ex- hay rotation - 1944 & '45. May 1943.

[1] Dimensions for 6.06 acres.
[2] Dimensions for 6.11 acres.
[3] Dimensions for 3.52 acres.

The foregoing data are indicated so that they may be used to evaluate other areas in relation to these from which runoff rates have been derived and thus serve as a guide for use in the application of the results.

For detailed information on topography, soils, slopes, erosion history, and cover or cropping procedures on the experimental areas see maps, *figures 12 to 22*, at the end of Part II of this publication. Pertinent descriptive information for the individual drainage areas is given in the text, pages 46 to 47 and 53 to 54. This information is deemed essential to the proper interpretation of the results from these studies.

INSTRUMENTATION AND COLLECTION OF RECORDS

The runoff measuring devices, consisting of broad-crested concrete weirs and sheet metal H-flumes and the precipitation stations for the various experimental areas are listed in *table 3*. Some of them are illustrated in *plates 1, 2, and 3*, pages 8, 9, and 10.

TABLE 3.—*Runoff and precipitation measuring stations on the experimental areas.*

Watershed designation and area acres	Runoff measuring stations			Precipitation measuring stations		
	Control type	Crest slope and head	Capacity c. f. s.	Designation	Recording capacity inches	Chart (clock cylinder revolves once)
FREEHOLD, N. J.						
Surgent (W-I) 15. 7 and 17.5	30-in. compound concr. weir[1]	3:1 (1ft.) 5:1(1.5 ft.)	102	R-1	6	in. 12 hours
Smith (W-II) 34.2 and 32.9	30-in. concrete weir	2:1 (3 ft.)	91	R-2 R-3	6 6	weekly in 12 hours
Sherrard (W-III) 51.8	30-in. concrete weir	2:1 (4.5 ft.)	286	R-4 R-5	6 6	weekly in 12 hours
Ward (W-IV) 102.7	30-in. concrete weir	5:1 (3.3 ft.)	320	R-6 R-7	6 6	weekly in 12 hours
UNIVERSITY OF MARYLAND—COLLEGE PARK, MD.						
W-I and W-II 8.22 and 7.44	16-in. concrete weirs (2)	3:1 (2.25 ft.)	65	R-1	[2]9 6	in 12 hours in 12 hours
W-III and W-IV [3]6.06 and [3]6.11	16-in. concrete weirs (2)	3:1 (2.5 ft.)	89	R-3	[2]9 6	in 12 hours in 12 hours
W-V (4.07)	H-3 flume	3 ft. head[4]	30.7	R-2	[2]6 9	weekly
W-VI and W-VII 3.53 and [3]3.52	H-3 flumes (2)	3 ft. head[4]	30.7	R-4	9	in 12 hours
W-VIII (2.43)	H-2.5 flume	2.5 ft. head[4]	19.4	S-6	USWB std.	non-recording
W-IX (12.05)	H-3 flume	3 ft. head[4]	30.7	R-8	9	in 12 hours
W-X (3.04)	H-3 flume	3 ft. head[4]	30.7	R-9	6	in 12 hours

[1]Compound crest slope, 3 feet horizontal on 1 foot vertical for 1 foot, then 5 on 1 for 1.5 feet.

[2]For 1939 and 1940 only.

[3]See table 2 for complete data on areas.

[4]Crest slope, 10-13/16 inches horizontal to 12 inches vertical.

Weirs and Flumes

The weirs and flumes were calibrated in the United States Bureau of Standards and Cornell University Hydraulic Laboratories, using one-tenth to full scale models. The characteristics of these measuring devices, rating tables for various approach channel conditions and structural details are fully described in a technical publication of the Soil Conservation Service.[6] All installations on the experimental areas covered in this report were designed for free flow conditions, and the effect of submergence (high tail-water levels) does not have to be considered, *see plate 2. B*. Slope factors for the concrete weirs were determined in all cases and corrections applied to the rating tables for the deviation of the actual weir from theoretical or laboratory dimensions. Back of several weirs, it was impossible to avoid considerable ponding due to flat gaging sites. Where necessary, rapidly rising hydrographs were corrected for this pondage which is a plus correction on rising stages and a minus correction on falling stages.[7] The flumes are constructed of galvanized sheet metal and angles to accurate dimensions and shape and have been maintained in proper adjustment. All flumes were installed in such a manner as to make the effect of pondage back of them negligible. In all cases, records of flow over the weirs and through the flumes were obtained with Friez FW-1 reversing, unlimited stage water-level recorders fitted with charts of sufficiently open scale to determine time to the nearest minute and gage heights to the nearest 0.01 foot. Laboratory tests of the flumes and weirs indicated accuracies within 1 percent or less. Under field conditions, however, the records may be considered to be within 5 percent.

Rain Gages

Friez recording non-reversing rain gages of 6- and 9-inch capacity were used to measure the rate and amount of precipitation. Open time scales (12-hr. charts on which 1 in. of chart equals 62 minutes of time) were used for recording the rain graphs in sufficient detail to determine time to the nearest minute and depths of precipitation to the nearest 0.01 inch. Some of the rain gages were equipped with weekly charts to facilitate the determination of dates and times of precipitation. All recording gage records were verified by a standard Weather Bureau gage placed 6 feet distant and at the same level. Recorder catches were also measured in the measuring tubes of the standard gages.

Meteorological Stations

Meteorological stations were located on the Smith (W-II) area at Freehold and on the W-I and W-IX areas at College Park. Air temperature, humidity, and soil temperatures at three depths were recorded on weekly charts. The readings of counting anemometers were taken on all visits to the areas to determine the total wind movement in miles. Air temperature was checked by maximum and minimum thermometers, soil temperatures by soil thermometers, and humidity by wet and dry bulb psychrometers.

Notes on Watershed Conditions

Records of time of plowing, planting, cultivating, and harvesting of crops, together with height and density of crops and cover, observations on erosion, snow cover, frost, and other watershed conditions were kept in field books, on maps or charts following standard procedures developed on a Nation-wide basis, and modified only where local conditions required it.

[6]HARROLD, L. L., and KRIMGOLD, D. B. DEVICES FOR MEASURING THE RATES AND AMOUNTS OF RUNOFF EMPLOYED IN SOIL CONSERVATION RESEARCH. U. S. Soil Conserv. Serv. Tech. Pub. 51, 42 pp., illus. July 1943. [Processed.]

[7]KRIMGOLD, D. B., and WEBER, J. L. PONDAGE CORRECTIONS INVOLVED IN MEASURING SURFACE RUNOFF FROM SMALL DRAINAGE BASINS. U. S. Soil Conserv. Serv. 18 pp., illus. November, 1939. [Mimeographed.]

A. Runoff from melting snow going over both weirs at gaging station W-I (8.22 acres) on right and W-II (7.44 acres) on left, April 1, 1942, at College Park. These are similar broad-crest concrete weirs 16 inches wide with 3 on 1 crest slopes, with a design capacity of 65 c. f. s., at a 2.25 foot head. Recorders for each watershed are mounted in shelter over separate 30-inch stilling wells. Two-foot overflow below notch of weirs. Flows shown were 0.11 c. f. s. on W-II (left) and 0.58 c. f. s. on W-I (right). Due to differences in exposure (aspect) W-II was only 25% bare of snow whereas W-I was 75% bare.

B. Double gaging station on 3.5-acre pastured watersheds W-VI left (no flow) and W-VII right (flow 0.05 c. f. s.) on April 1, 1942. W-VI was 50% bare of snow and W-VII was 80% bare. Measuring devices are H-3 flumes made of galvanized sheet metal reinforced with angles. They each have a rated capacity of 30.7 c. f. s. Each shelter contains a water-level recorder mounted over a 9-inch stilling well attached to the side of the flume.

PLATE 2

NJ-30,415

A, View looking downstream toward the weir and gaging station (W-II) on the T. Smith farm near Freehold, N. J. It was taken on June 23, 1938, just after the peak flow of 54.6 cubic feet per second or 1.56 inches per hour from 34.2 acres. This runoff peak ranked second in the 6 years of records. Debris on the staff gage opposite the instrument shelter is a rough indication of the maximum flow level at weir.

NJ-30,416

B, Picture of the flow from below the control weir taken a few minutes after view above. Free flow conditions exist at all discharges due to a drop of 2 feet from the weir notch to the apron floor below. Note the heavy concentration of silt in the muddy runoff water. This resulted from the off-contour tillage on the drainage area above.

0

PLATE 3

A. Typical precipitation measuring station R-1 near Freehold, N. J. It consists of a standard Weather Bureau rain gage on left, located 6 feet from
the recording rain gage, all inside a fence enclosure. In the background
is the Surgent (W-I) weir and instrument shelter at the lower end of the
terrace-outlet channel.

B. W-III runoff gaging station on J. Sherrard farm near Freehold, N. J., on
September 12, 1939. Weir crest has a slope of 2 horizontal on 1 vertical.
Face gage on weir and two staff gages at left are used to check water level
as recorded by Fries FW-1 recorder in well. Water enters the 36-inch stilling well through 1-inch holes in intake plank 10 feet back of weir. This
watershed flows continuously. Base flow shown is 0.003 c. f. s. at 0.08
foot head, or 0.0015 inch of runoff daily. Rainfall Station R-4 in background.

Records

Tabulation, computation, and compilation of the data were accomplished by following standard procedures. In this way the data meet certain minimum requirements of uniformity and can be compared with similar data from other regions and localities.

RATES OF RUNOFF FOR THE DESIGN OF CONSERVATION STRUCTURES

Criteria for Design

In designing small conservation and other structures it should be recognized that changes in land use are apt to be made during the life of the structure. Cropping lay-outs existing at the time a structure or practice is being planned may not be followed in the future. Circumstances may require a farmer to change his farming operations which would increase the proportion of land in cultivated crops. Meadows or pastures may be plowed up and cropped. Furthermore, ownership of the land may change and a new type of farm enterprise be placed upon the land. Due to these, and other uncertainties, it is necessary to assume conditions that will produce the higher rates of runoff where it is reasonable to expect such changes to occur during the economic life of the structure.

For example, in laying out a diversion terrace on a pasture which has plowable land, it is advisable to design it for runoff from cultivated land rather than that from pasture. On the other hand, if the pasture is steep, rough, rocky, or stumpy, or contains considerable brush or trees, or is poorly drained, and for these reasons not likely to be plowed, it would not be reasonable to design the capacity of the diversion channel on the basis of runoff from cultivated land. In making this decision the designer should keep in mind that, in the case of structures on small drainage areas, small differences in the assumed rates of runoff would result in practically negligible changes in cost of the structure.

The results of the analyses of the experimental data, modified by considerations of changing land use, form the basis for the graphs and tabulations presented in this report for use in determining capacities of spillways, culverts, diversion channels and outlets, terrace-outlet channels, and similar structures on small watersheds. Values for drainage areas up to 40 acres are presented in *tables 4 to 8*, pages 14 to 17. Rates of runoff for larger areas are given in the form of curves in *figures 2, 3, 4, and 5*, pages 18 to 21. The tables are intended for use with the smaller structures, the planning and lay-out of which are usually entrusted to field personnel of limited qualifications. The curves which apply to the larger areas involve large flows and should be used by engineers and technicians of higher training and experience. The tables and graphs have been so designed that they can be incorporated in handbooks or instructions of such agencies as the Soil Conservation Service, Production and Marketing Administration, State and local highway departments, and of other agencies concerned with the planning, financing, and construction of structures and conservation practices on small drainage areas. A description of the methodology followed in preparing these tables and graphs will be found in Part II of this report.

Frequency of Recurrence in Years

The values given in the graphs and tabulations are those that may be expected to be equaled or exceeded once in 10 years. It is assumed that small structures on areas of less than 40 acres need not be designed for higher values or recurrences. Structures on larger areas covered by the curves may, under certain conditions be designed to carry runoffs which can, on the average, be expected to be equaled or exceeded once in 25 years. When this is desired, the coefficient or multiplier given in the body of the graph should be applied to the values shown by the curves.

The statement that a value has a 10-year frequency of recurrence means that the value will be equaled or exceeded on the average of 10 times in 100 years. It does not mean that it will be exceeded or equaled in every 10-year period but the chances are that on the average it will be 10 times in a century. A 25-year frequency of recurrence would be equaled or exceeded 4 times in 100 years. In a given 10-year period it is possible to have two or more 10-year runoffs and even a 25-year flow. It is also possible that there would be no 10- or 25-year flows. If a structure overflows or exceeds its capacity once or twice, it does not necessarily mean that it is under-designed; it means that it experienced runoffs of a higher recurrence value than that for which it was designed. Such events must be expected to occur occasionally. However, if a structure overtops habitually, it may be under-designed for the conditions under which it operates. The above conceptions should be kept in mind in evaluating the adequacy of structures or practices.

Limitations in Application of the Data

The attention of prospective users of these data is called particularly to the statements in the tables and on the graphs describing the conditions to which the values are applicable. *The use of these values in cases other than those described would result in either too frequent failures or in uneconomical design and would defeat the whole purpose of this publication.*

The values shown in the graphs and tabulations are based upon soil conditions summarized in *tables 1 and 2*, pages 4 and 5, and shown on maps in *figures 12, 14, 15, 16*, pages 48 to 52, and *figures 17, 19, 21, and 22*, pages 55 to 60, under the heading, 'Detailed Descriptions of the Experimental Areas,' Part II of this report. These soil conditions fall into three general categories:

(1) *Light-textured, deep (36 in. or more), well-drained soils.*

(2) *Light- to medium-textured, moderately deep (20 to 36 in.), imperfectly drained.*

(3) *Medium-textured, shallow (10 to 20 in.), imperfectly drained.*

The permeability factor was considered in setting up these categories. It was concluded that permeability as the term would be understood by the users of the runoff data is amply expressed by the terms used in describing texture and drainage conditions (well-drained, imperfectly drained). It is believed that the descriptions used will be understandable to workers if they remember that the 'textures' indicated apply to the hydrologic behavior of the whole profile (not the surface soil alone).

Curves and design tables are *not* intended to apply to flat or swampy lands or to drainage areas containing appreciable portions of such lands. They *do* apply to *sloping land* in the Coastal Plains of New Jersey, Delaware, and Maryland. The slopes and configurations of the experimental areas from which the runoff data have been derived are typical of the sloping lands in the Coastal Plains, and the data can be applied directly to them when the soil conditions are similar. The three categories mentioned above do not represent all the soil conditions that are encountered in the area of recommended application (see map on cover), and application of the results to other conditions should be made with caution.

Table 7, page 17, was prepared for use in the design of single vegetated diversion terraces with a grass filter strip at least 20 feet wide above the terrace channel. *It should only be applied to diversions with more than 160 feet of terrace per acre of drainage area.* The matter of concentration of water above the proposed terrace channel should also be studied. If there are no serious concentrations of water along the site, the rates in *table 7* may be used. If well-defined natural waterways concentrate the flow from the area above in one or two spots, the channel storage of the diversion channel would not be sufficiently effective in reducing the peak flow. In such cases values given in *tables 4, 5, or 8*, pages 14, 15, and 17, should be used depending on whether the land above is likely to be cultivated or is in pasture or woods.

For woodlands, in the absence of conclusive proof, the effects of litter and canopy are deemed the dominant factors, and soil condition, a lesser factor. Thus the woodland curves in *figure 5*, page 21, and design *table 8*, page 17, are based on the cover and litter rather than on soil conditions, and particular care should be devoted to evaluating the character of the woodland in applying the data, *see plate 4*, page 22. Curve 'B' in *figure 5* is only given for areas up to 40 acres because mature stands of timber under proper woodland management seldom are found on areas exceeding 40 acres.

TABLE 4.--*Rates of runoff[1] for design of conservation structures on cultivated land and on land likely to be cultivated in the Coastal Plains of New Jersey, Delaware, and Maryland.*

The rates shown in this table do not apply to CROPLAND TERRACES or to DIVERSION TERRACES. See tables 6 and 7.

Drainage area	Rate of runoff		Drainage area	Rate of runoff	
	Case "A"[2]	Case "B"[3]		Case "A"[2]	Case "B"[3]
acres.	c. f. s.	c. f. s.	acres.	c. f. s.	c. f. s.
2	15	19	22	77	105
3	20	25	23	80	108
4	24	31	24	83	111
5	28	36	25	85	114
6	32	41	26	87	118
7	36	46	27	90	121
8	39	50	28	92	124
9	42	55	29	94	127
10	45	59	30	96	130
11	48	63	31	98	133
12	51	66	32	101	135
13	54	70	33	103	139
14	57	74	34	105	141
15	60	78	35	107	144
16	62	81	36	109	146
17	65	85	37	111	150
18	68	88	38	113	152
19	71	92	39	115	155
20	73	95	40	117	157
21	75	102			

[1] Based on 10-year frequency of recurrence, 100 percent row crops, off-contour.

[2] CASE 'A' applies to sloping land with light-textured, deep, well-drained soils such as Chillum, Collington, Freehold, Sassafras, and Hyattsville loams; Freehold, Sassafras, and Collington sandy loams; and similar soils.

[3] CASE 'B' applies to sloping land with medium-textured, imperfectly drained soils underlain by a very slowly permeable hardpan at a depth of about 25 inches, such as Beltsville silt loam, loam, gravelly silt loam, and gravelly loam; and similar soils.

TABLE 5.--*Rates of runoff[1] for design of conservation structures on pastures in the Coastal Plains of New Jersey, Delaware, and Maryland.*

The rates shown in this table should be used only for rocky, stumpy, and other pastures which are not likely to be cultivated. Use table 4 for pastures likely to be cultivated.

Drainage area	Rate of runoff		Drainage area	Rate of runoff	
	Case "A"[2]	Case "B"[3]		Case "A"[2]	Case "B"[3]
acres.	*c. f. s.*	*c. f. s.*	*acres.*	*c. f. s.*	*c. f. s.*
2	7	9	22	38	48
3	9	12	23	39	50
4	12	15	24	40	52
5	14	18	25	41	53
6	15	20	26	43	55
7	17	22	27	44	57
8	19	24	28	45	58
9	20	26	29	46	59
10	22	28	30	47	61
11	23	30	31	48	62
12	25	32	32	49	63
13	26	34	33	50	64
14	28	36	34	51	66
15	29	37	35	52	67
16	30	39	36	53	68
17	32	41	37	54	69
18	33	43	38	55	71
19	34	44	39	56	72
20	35	46	40	57	73
21	37	47			

[1]Based on 10-year frequency of recurrence, on permanent pastures or long term meadows.

[2]CASE 'A' applies to sloping land with light-textured, deep, well-drained soils such as Chillum, Collington, Freehold, Sassafras, and Hyattsville loams; Freehold, Sassafras, and Collington sandy loams; and similar soils.

[3]CASE 'B' applies to sloping land with medium-textured, imperfectly drained soils underlain by a very slowly permeable hardpan at a depth of about 25 inches, such as Beltsville silt loam, loam, gravelly silt loam, and gravelly loam; and similar soils.

TABLE 6.--*Rates of runoff[1] for design of outlet channels from terraced fields of 4 to 40 acres in size in the Coastal Plains of New Jersey, Delaware, and Maryland.*

CASE 'A' applies to light-textured, deep, well-drained soils such as Collington, Freehold, Sassafras, and Chillum sandy loams and loams; and similar soils

Drainage area	Average length of cropland terraces in feet														
	400	500	600	700	800	900	1000	1100	1200	1300	1400	1500	1600	1800	2000
acres	Runoff in cubic feet per second[2]														
4	10	10	9	9	9	8	8	8	8	8	7	7	7	7	7
6	15	15	14	13	13	13	12	12	12	11	11	11	11	10	10
.8	20	19	19	18	17	17	16	16	15	15	15	14	14	14	13
10	26	24	23	22	22	21	20	20	19	19	18	18	18	17	16
12	31	29	28	27	26	25	24	24	23	23	22	22	21	20	20
14	36	34	32	31	30	29	28	28	27	26	26	25	25	24	23
16	41	39	37	36	35	34	32	32	31	30	29	29	28	27	26
18	46	44	42	40	39	38	37	35	35	34	33	32	32	30	29
20	51	48	46	45	43	42	41	39	38	38	37	36	35	34	33
24	61	58	56	54	52	50	49	47	46	45	44	43	42	41	39
28	71	68	65	63	60	59	57	55	54	53	51	50	49	47	46
32	82	77	74	72	69	67	65	63	61	60	59	58	56	54	52
36	92	87	84	80	78	75	73	71	69	68	66	65	63	61	59
40	102	97	93	89	86	84	81	79	77	75	73	72	70	68	65

CASE 'B' applies to medium to light-textured, moderately deep, imperfectly drained soils such as gravelly loams, sandy loams, fine sandy loams, and loams of the Beltsville series; and similar soils.

Drainage area	Average length of cropland terraces in feet														
	400	500	600	700	800	900	1000	1100	1200	1300	1400	1500	1600	1800	2000
acres	Runoff in cubic feet per second[2]														
4	12	11	11	10	10	10	9	9	9	9	8	8	8	8	7
6	18	17	16	15	15	14	14	14	13	13	13	12	12	12	11
.8	23	22	21	21	20	19	19	18	18	17	17	16	16	16	15
10	29	28	27	26	25	24	23	23	22	22	21	21	20	19	19
12	35	33	32	31	30	29	28	27	26	26	25	25	24	23	22
14	41	39	37	36	35	34	33	32	31	30	30	29	28	27	26
16	47	44	43	41	40	38	37	36	35	34	34	33	32	31	30
18	53	50	48	46	45	43	42	41	40	39	38	37	36	35	34
20	59	56	53	51	50	48	47	45	44	43	42	41	40	39	37
24	70	67	64	62	60	58	56	54	53	52	51	49	48	47	45
28	82	78	74	72	69	67	65	63	62	60	59	58	57	54	52
32	94	89	85	82	79	77	75	72	70	69	68	66	65	62	60
36	105	100	96	92	89	86	84	82	79	77	76	74	73	70	67
40	117	111	106	103	99	96	93	91	88	86	84	82	81	78	75

[1]Based on 10-year frequency of recurrence, 100 percent row crops, contour-tilled.

[2]The values given in these tables apply to terraced areas with a vertical spacing[3] equal to: $\dfrac{\text{Slope of land (in percent)}}{3} + 2$.

[3]In feet.

TABLE 7.--*Rates of runoff[1] for design of diversion terraces on cultivated land in the Coastal Plains of New Jersey, Delaware, and Maryland.*

Values in this table apply to standard DIVERSION TERRACES protected by a grass strip, and having more than 160 feet of terrace per acre of drainage area, and WITHOUT DEFINITE NATURAL WATERWAYS. For areas WITH WELL-DEFINED WATERWAYS use tables 4, 5, or 8.

Drainage area	Rate of runoff		Drainage area	Rate of runoff	
	Case "A"[2]	Case "B"[3]		Case "A"[2]	Case "B"[3]
acres	c. f. s.	c. f. s.	acres	c. f. s.	c. f. s.
2	6	8	9	18	23
3	8	11	10	19	25
4	10	13	11	20	27
5	12	15	12	22	28
6	13	17	13	23	30
7	15	19	14	24	31
8	16	20	15	25	33

[1]Based on 10-year frequency of recurrence, 100 percent row crops, contour-tilled.

[2]CASE 'A' applies to sloping land with light-textured, deep, well-drained soils such as Collington, Freehold, and Sassafras sandy loams; Collington, Freehold, Sassafras, Hyattsville, and Chillum loams; and similar soils.

[3]CASE 'B' applies to sloping land with medium-textured, imperfectly drained soils, underlain by a very slowly permeable hardpan at a depth of about 25 inches, such as Beltsville gravelly loam, gravelly silt loam, silt loam, and loam; and similar soils.

TABLE 8.--*Rates of runoff[1] for design of conservation structures on woodland in the Coastal Plains of New Jersey, Delaware, and Maryland.*

Drainage area	Rate of runoff		Drainage area	Rate of runoff	
	Case "A"[2]	Case "B"[3]		Case "A"[2]	Case "B"[3]
acres	c. f. s.	c. f. s.	acres	c. f. s.	c. f. s.
2	2	1	18	8	4
4	3	1	20	8	4
6	3	2	22	9	4
8	4	2	24	10	4
10	5	2	28	11	5
12	6	3	32	12	5
14	6	3	36	13	6
16	7	3	40	14	6

[1]Based on 10-year frequency of recurrence.

[2]CASE 'A' applies to sloping, ungrazed, cut-over, deciduous woodland with a poor canopy and uneven litter with bare spots characteristic of such woodland. (Pl. 4, A, p. 22.)

[3]CASE 'B' applies to sloping, ungrazed, undisturbed, deciduous woodland with a good canopy and a good uniform litter. (See pl. 4, B.)

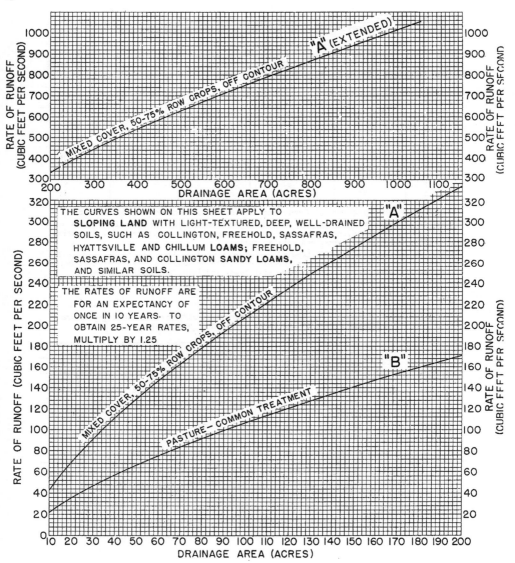

FIGURE 2.–RATES OF RUNOFF FOR DESIGN OF CONSERVATION STRUCTURES ON SLOPING
LAND WITH LIGHT-TEXTURED, DEEP, WELL-DRAINED SOILS IN THE COASTAL PLAINS
OF NEW JERSEY, DELAWARE, AND MARYLAND.

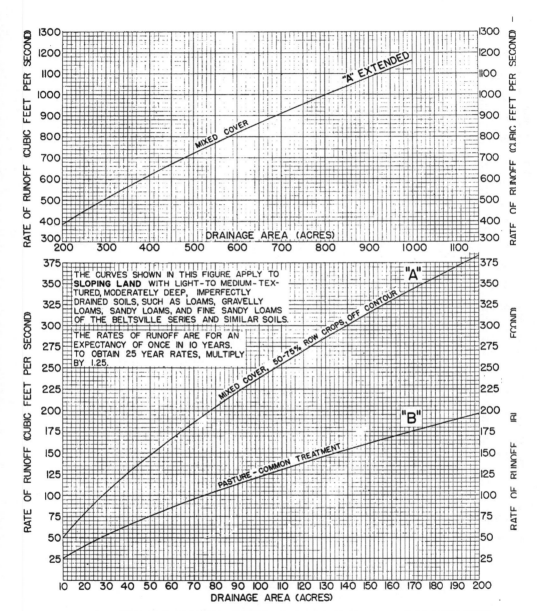

FIGURE 3.- **RATES OF RUNOFF FOR DESIGN** OF CONSERVATION STRUCTURES ON **SLOPING
LANDS** OF **MEDIUM-TO LIGHT-TEXTURED, MODERATELY DEEP, IMPERFECTLY
DRAINED** SOILS IN THE **COASTAL PLAINS** OF **NEW JERSEY, DELAWARE,** AND
MARYLAND.

SOIL CONSERVATION SERVICE, WASHINGTON, D.C
APRIL 1946

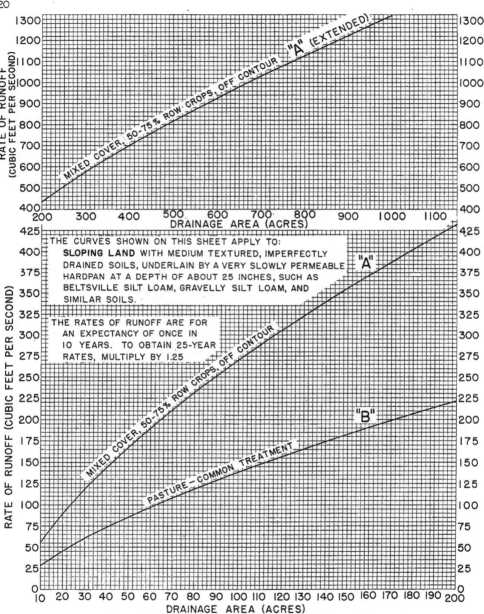

FIGURE 4.—RATES OF RUNOFF FOR DESIGN OF CONSERVATION STRUCTURES ON **SLOPING
LAND** OF **MEDIUM-TEXTURED, SHALLOW, IMPERFECTLY-DRAINED** SOILS IN THE
COASTAL PLAINS OF NEW JERSEY, DELAWARE, AND MARYLAND.

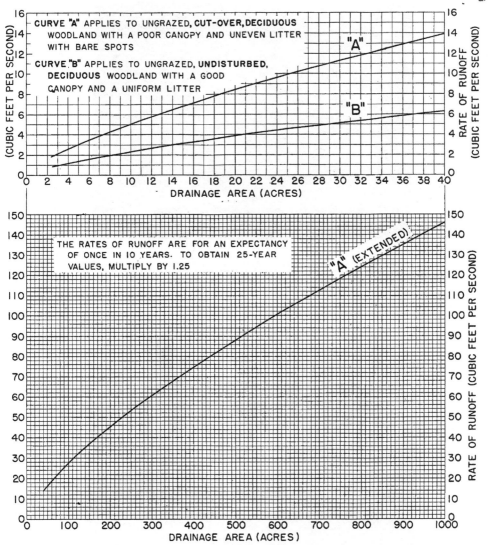

FIGURE 5 – RATES OF RUNOFF FOR DESIGN OF CONSERVATION STRUCTURES ON SLOPING WOODLANDS IN THE COASTAL PLAINS OF NEW JERSEY, DELAWARE, AND MARYLAND.

SOIL CONSERVATION SERVICE, WASHINGTON, D C
APRIL 1948

2

_A_, Ungrazed, cut-over, largely deciduous woodland with a thin and variable canopy, uneven ground litter with frequent bare areas and an actual history of ground fires (W-VIII College Park, Md., 2.43 acres).

_B_, Ungrazed, unburned, undisturbed, largely deciduous woodland with a high uniform canopy and an excellent litter on the forest floor (W-IX College Park, Md., 12.05 acres).

PART II

METHODS USED TO DETERMINE DESIGN VALUES OF RUNOFF RATES

Records of runoff from small agricultural watersheds for periods of 5 or 6 years are far from sufficient for an adequate analysis. However, since there is no prospect of adding to the length of the runoff records from the Freehold, N. J., watersheds (discontinued Oct. 1943) and further, since there exists an urgent need for even provisional information on runoff rates for the rapidly expanding soil conservation districts' program, as well as for the activities of the other agencies, it has been deemed advisable to study the records now available and extract therefrom as many usable results as the limited data will allow.

To accomplish the above objective, it was not always possible to secure adequate proofs for the indicated results. Some of the conclusions that were reached and the derived curves and values obtained may not be as well supported as they could have been if longer records were available and more ideal size and other watershed characteristics had existed on the experimental areas. These limitations must be kept in mind in considering the following discussions and results.

Comparison of Rainfall Intensities

Estimates of future hydrologic events can best be made by assuming that what has happened in the past is representative of what is likely to occur in the future. The value of the estimate depends on the length of the past record. When long runoff records are non-existent, it is necessary to check the available short record in all possible ways to ascertain whether it constitutes a fair sample of longer records. It is not always possible to test it with respect to many of the watershed factors. However, the rainfall intensities recorded during the period of investigation can be compared with the longer records which are available for College Park, Md., and Freehold, N. J.[8] Rainfall depths in inches were interpolated between the lines of equal precipitation (isohyetals) on the Yarnell frequency-intensity maps for the College Park and Freehold locations. For short durations, these values are somewhat lower than the actual depths, because they were determined from the Weather Bureau tabulations based on uniform 5-minute intervals. To make them comparable with the records tabulated from weighing type rain gages used in our investigations, where the actual changes or 'breaks' in the rain graph are taken, the Yarnell depths were increased by 10, 7, and 5 percent for 10-, 30-, and 60-minute durations, respectively. These modified depths were then converted to intensities in inches per hour.

TABLE 9.--*Comparison of 10- and 25-year values of rainfall intensities in inches per hour derived from Freehold, N. J., and College Park, Md., records with modified Yarnell values.*

Duration minutes	Modified Yarnell (Misc. Pub.No.204)			R-1, on Surgent (W-I) N.J.(1938-43)		
	10-year	25-year	Ratio 10/25	10-year	25 year	Ratio 10/25
	FREEHOLD, N. J.					
10	6.27	7.15	1.14	6.20	6.75	1.09
30	3.75	4.47	1.19	3.25	3.65	1.12
60	2.25	2.84	1.26	2.03	2.35	1.16
	COLLEGE PARK, MD.					
	Modified Yarnell (Misc. Pub.No.204)			R-1, on W-I and W-II, Md. (1939-45)		
10	6.33	7.21	1.14	6.60	7.25	1.10
30	3.72	4.37	1.17	3.50	4.10	1.17
60	2.36	2.84	1.20	1.65	1.80	1.09

[8]See footnote 5, p. 1.

From the table on the preceding page, it appears that the rainfall intensities experienced in the 6-year periods at Freehold and College Park were slightly below Yarnell's modified values for 10-minute durations at Freehold and slightly above for College Park. The 30-minute durations were somewhat below Yarnell's at both locations. The 60-minute rates for 10 and 25 years fall considerably below Yarnell's expectancies, particularly at College Park. However, since the periods of rise of the hydrographs for the most significant storms on all the watersheds are all less than 30 minutes, in fact average closer to 10 than 30 minutes, it has been assumed that the 10-minute durations are best for judging the periods of record. It therefore appears that insofar as intensities of rainfall are concerned, the peak rates of runoff recorded at both locations can be considered a fair sample of longer periods.

It should be noted further that the rainfall rates for the 10- and 30-minute durations judged either from Yarnell's values or the actual rates are quite similar for the two locations. This means that rainfall rates to be expected at Freehold are not significantly different from those to be anticipated at College Park. Within the Coastal Plains area, therefore, similar rainfall rates occur and it is reasonable to assume that similar rates of runoff will occur. It is unnecessary to apply a rainfall-rate factor to any portion of the area, and the estimated runoff rates derived for either the Freehold or College Park areas are interchangeable without modification, as far as climatological factors are concerned.

Peak Rate vs Drainage Area Relationships

The determination of the design rates of runoff already presented, as well as the study of the effects of various factors on runoff rates discussed later, involves the relationship between the peak rates of runoff and the size or area of the watershed. The relationship could probably be best studied by the analysis of long time records from drainage areas of various sizes, but with similar shapes, soils, and cultural practices. Such records are not available for the Coastal Plains area. However, it was felt that an indication of this relationship could be gained from a study of the concurrent peaks on some of the College Park and Freehold watersheds.

The two pairs of watersheds at College Park were therefore selected for study during the periods when they were in common pasture. Combinations were made of concurrent individual runoffs from two adjacent pastures to get the maximum runoff peak from the simultaneous flows of the two. These combined peaks then were compared with the peaks of one of the areas by plotting on semi-log paper against the corresponding drainage areas and drawing straight lines through the points. Generally the maximum storms were taken, if investigation showed that conditions were comparable on the two areas at that time. Area-factor curves derived for the 7.05- and 3.53-acre areas (W-VI + W-VII to W-VI) and the 13.67- and 8.01-acre areas (W-III + W-IV to W-IV) checked closely, thus giving an area-factor curve for a range of about 2 to 50 acres. For areas above this range, Smith (32.9 acres) and Ward (102.7 acres) watersheds at Freehold were selected as being most similar in soils, shape, and cover conditions. Each area had about 75 percent row crops off-contour, and the rest was mixed cover. The watersheds are located 2.5 miles apart, so a careful study was made of concurrent conditions on the watersheds and of the similarity of the intensity and amounts of rainfall. A number of significant runoff rates were plotted on semi-log paper and the pair of points selected that gave the most reasonable area-factor curve. This curve was superimposed on that already tentatively derived from the College Park areas. These two curves agreed closely for areas up to 30 acres, but for areas greater than 30 acres the College Park curve gave lower size factors than the Freehold curve. A composite curve was then constructed, based largely on College Park factors up to 30 acres and on the Freehold values up to 200 acres. Through a study of rates of runoff recorded by the United States Geological Survey on July 2 to 4, 1942, on five drainage areas lying within the Coastal Plains, the composite curve was extended to 1,000 acres. These USGS drainage basins were large, ranging from 45 to 71 square miles in area.

With a peak rate-drainage area relationship thus established, the next operation was to determine for the several experimental watersheds and the conditions represented by them the limits of peak rates of runoff for various frequencies of recurrence. These rates of runoff, together with the rate-area relationship form the basis for the preceding *tables 4 to 8*, inclusive, pages 14 to 17, and *figures 2, 3, 4, and 5*, pages 18 to 21.

Frequency of Recurrence of Runoff Peaks

Many attempts have been made to evaluate the frequency of recurrence of rainfall intensities and multiply these rates by an overall coefficient representing all other watershed factors to arrive at runoff rates of a specified frequency for given cases. Such procedures have been reasonably successful in storm sewer and similar designs, when applied to highly developed urban areas, which drain largely impervious roofs, pavements, walks, driveways, etc., with a minimum of grassed or landscaped area. When the proportion of more pervious or variable conditions increases, however, the limitation of the method is soon reached. Intensities and amounts of rainfall are only two of the many factors that affect the magnitude and frequency of runoff peaks. Among these other factors are: The available moisture-holding capacity of the soil profiles; permeability of the whole profile or rate of water movement through the soil column; surface infiltration opportunities of the soil surface and its vegetal cover, if any; texture, structure, depth, and tilth of the soil; configuration, shape, and degree of dissection (drainage density) of the contributing area; grades, shape, friction factors, and other hydraulic characteristics of the channels and watercourses; height and density of vegetal cover; direction and manner of tillage; sequence of or location of various crops on the area from year to year; size and velocity of raindrops; inclination and direction of rainfall; turbulence of surface winds; temperature of soil and air particularly as reflected in frost, sleet, and snow conditions; and exposure (aspect) of the area. The length of the above list of other factors affecting surface runoff makes it evident that the frequency of recurrence of runoff peaks cannot be determined by the simple application of a factor to rainfall rates.

The many factors mentioned in the foregoing paragraph and described in a previously published paper[9] indicate that the smaller peaks on a given area are the result of combinations of factors that occur rather frequently on the area. The larger runoff peaks are produced by rarer composites of conditions that happen much less frequently. It is believed far more expedient and logical to work directly with runoff records in estimating frequency of recurrence of runoff rates than in the indirect method of rainfall intensities.

For the determination of frequency of recurrence of peak rates of runoff for various land-use practices, as well as maximum rainfall intensities for a given time interval, the duration-curve method was used.[10] The method of maximum annual runoff peaks (one value per year of record) was considered to be too small and too uncertain a sample (3 to 6 values) of the short term data to give satisfactory frequencies. In some cases, the method produced fairly good results if the few values in the sample happened to be well distributed in magnitude. In the duration-curve procedure, all runoff peaks in a particular record above a selected minimum value were taken. This minimum value was set low enough to provide 30 to 50 peaks for analysis. These were arranged in order of

[9]HOBBS, H. W. RUNOFF BEHAVIOR OF SMALL AGRICULTURAL WATERSHEDS UNDER VARIOUS LAND USE PRACTICES. Amer. Geophy. Union. Trans. 27: pp. 69-80, 889-894, illus. 1946.

[10]HAZEN, ALLEN. FLOOD FLOWS: A STUDY OF FREQUENCIES AND MAGNITUDES, pp. 106-112, John Wiley and Sons, New York. 1930.

magnitude and the average number of times per annum that peaks above a certain limit occurred were computed using the following formulas:

$$P = \frac{2m - 1}{2n} \cdot \cdot \cdot \cdot \cdot \cdot \cdot \cdot \cdot \cdot \cdot \cdot \cdot \cdot \cdot \cdot \cdot \cdot \quad (1)$$

$$P = \frac{m}{n} \cdot \cdot \cdot \cdot \cdot \cdot \cdot \cdot \cdot \cdot \cdot \cdot \cdot \cdot \cdot \cdot \cdot \cdot \quad (2)$$

In which

P = the plotting position in terms. of the number of times per. annum,
m = the.order number of terms. after. they were arranged in descending magnitude, and
n = the number. of years. of record.

The data were plotted on Hazen's modified (expanded)[11] log-probability paper and on log-log paper and smooth curves drawn in graphically through or among the points, as illustrated in *figure 6*, page 27. The peak that would occur on the average of once per year was considered to have a 1-year frequency of recurrence and the 0.1 peak a 10-year frequency. In other words, the reciprocal of the plotting positions gave the recurrence interval in years, so that for a 6-year record the frequency of recurrence of the highest value *(m = 1)* was 12 years for equation (1) and 6 years for equation (2).

The longest records available were used to estimate peak rates of runoff for frequencies of recurrence of 10 and 25 years. The curves drawn through the *m/n* plottings generally gave the higher values, and these were used in the preparation of the tables and graphs.

Relationships were determined for pairs of nearby or adjacent areas by log-log or linear plotting of concurrent peak runoff rates when rainfall, soil moisture, and most other conditions were similar, but one factor was different, such as, soil condition or tillage direction, etc. If the areas were of different size, the rates of one were adjusted to the other by applying appropriate area factors before plotting. Lines or curves were fitted to the most significant of the array of points and ratios of the peaks determined. These ratios were then used to modify the 10-year rates of runoff derived for the check areas (that is, those with the longest records) to get 10-year rates for the conditions in which the record was too short for the direct determination of frequency of recurrence. In some cases diagrams similar to the lower graph in *figure 11*, page 44, were also prepared and utilized for determining peak ratios.

Using the 10-year rates of runoff for given areas and conditions derived by the procedures just discussed, and the area factors from the composite peak rate-drainage area relationship curve, the 10-year design rates were extended in both directions and the curves shown in *figures 2 to 5*, inclusive, pages 18 to 21, were obtained for areas of from 2 to 200 or 1,000 acres. From a study of the relationships of 10-year rates to 25-year rates, it was found that if the 10-year values were multiplied by 1.25, safe 25-year values can be obtained. A similar procedure was used in determining the estimated 10-year rates of runoff shown in *figures 7 to 9*, pages 29 to 31, for 2 to 20 acres (except for diversion terraces only to 15 acres).

---

[11]See footnotes 9 and 10, p. 25.

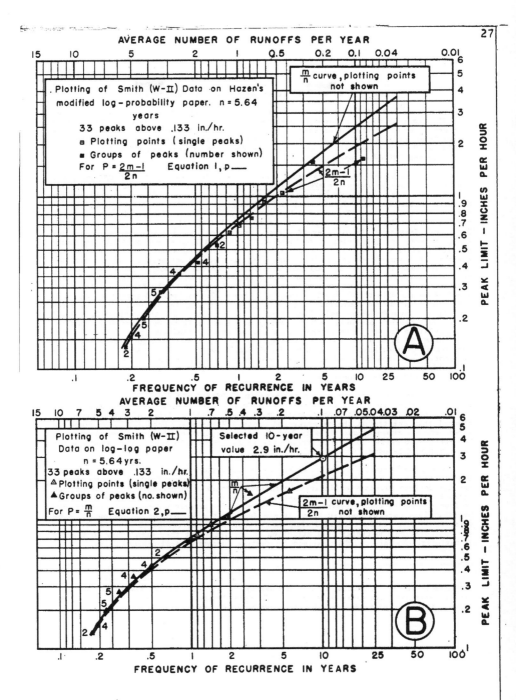

_FIGURE 6.--Methods of estimating peak rates of runoff from Smith W-II Records, Freehold, N. J.

Use of Figures 7 to 10 as Basis for Design Tables

It is not intended that the curves of estimated rates of runoff shown in *figures 7 to 10*, pages 29 to 32, be used in the field in selecting design values. *Tables 4 to 8*, pages 14 to 17, derived from these curves, serve that purpose. The derivation of the curves shown in *figure 10*, as well as the use made of these curves and some of those in *figures 7, 8, and 9* in arriving at the design values given in *tables 6 and 7*, are discussed in the following paragraphs.

Figure 10 shows 10-year rates of runoff in *cubic feet per second per acre* for standard cropland terraces for *average lengths* of all the terraces in the system of from 400 to 2,000 feet. It should be remembered that runoff from individual terraces was not measured on the Surgent W-I watershed at Freehold, but only the total flow from the nine terraces in the system. There were, however, values available for standard terraces of varying lengths derived from records of runoff from individual terraces at the Blacklands Experiment Station at Temple, Tex.[12] Since the vertical spacing and channel grades for these terraces are quite similar to those on the Surgent farm at Freehold, the hydraulic characteristics of the terrace systems are comparable and should produce comparable runoffs. Ten-year rates of runoff in cubic feet per second per acre for single terraces of varying lengths of 800 to 2,000 feet were taken from the Blacklands report and plotted on semi-log paper (terrace length on log scale and rate on linear scale). From this, factors for various terrace lengths were derived and applied to the Freehold rate corresponding to a length of 600 feet. Curve 'A', *figure 10*, resulted and served as the basis for Case 'A' in *table 6* expressed in *cubic feet per second* for various areas in acres (for light-textured, deep, well-drained soils). For curve 'B', the College Park W-III (deep, well-drained pasture) to W-VI (moderately deep, well to imperfectly drained pasture) relation for soil conditions during a concurrent period was applied to the Freehold curve 'A' data to get 10-year rates for medium- to light-textured, moderately deep, imperfectly drained soils. Thus curve 'B' of *figure 10* (Case 'B' of *table 6*) is the best information now available and will have to serve for terrace-outlet design for this soil condition until such time as a research study on cropland terraces located on imperfectly drained soils is undertaken.

The curve values for diversion terraces in *figures 7 and 9* were increased 25 to 30 percent in order to arrive at values for *table 7*. This was to allow for larger percentages of cultivated land or slightly more small concentrations of water above the channel than existed on the experimental areas W-V and W-X. Drainage areas above 15 acres were not shown because this is beyond the upper limit of what one diversion should be expected to carry. If the drainage area is larger than 15 acres, more than one diversion should be used.

Curves for pasture furrows on light- to medium-textured, moderately deep to shallow, imperfectly drained soils were not shown separately on *figures 8 and 9*. Experimental results derived directly or indirectly indicated about a 40 percent reduction in peak rates below the curves for common pasture treatment. *(See fig. 11 and discussion of contour furrows vs common pasture, p. 43)* Allowing for deterioration in the furrows and possibly less careful construction, it was felt that a 30 percent reduction would be safer, and these values coincided with the diversion-terrace curves 'D' in *figures 8 and 9*. Footnotes on the charts call attention to the fact that they also apply to furrows in pastures. No data could be derived for pasture furrows on well-drained soils.

---

[12] HARROLD, L. L., KRIMGOLD, D. B., and WESTBY, L. A. PRELIMINARY REPORT ON WATERSHED STUDIES NEAR WACO AND GARLAND, TEXAS. U. S. Soil Conserv. Serv. Tech. Pub. 53, 22 pp. illus. 1944. [Processed. See 10-year curve on lower graph, *fig. 3*, p. 7.]

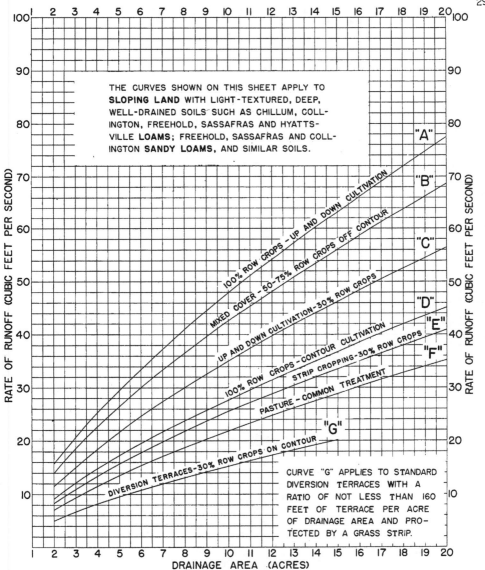

THE CURVES SHOWN ON THIS SHEET APPLY TO
SLOPING LAND WITH LIGHT-TEXTURED, DEEP,
WELL-DRAINED SOILS SUCH AS CHILLUM, COLL-
INGTON, FREEHOLD, SASSAFRAS AND HYATTS-
VILLE **LOAMS**; FREEHOLD, SASSAFRAS AND COLL-
INGTON **SANDY LOAMS**, AND SIMILAR SOILS.

CURVE "G" APPLIES TO STANDARD
DIVERSION TERRACES WITH A
RATIO OF NOT LESS THAN 160
FEET OF TERRACE PER ACRE
OF DRAINAGE AREA AND PRO-
TECTED BY A GRASS STRIP.

RATE OF RUNOFF (CUBIC FEET PER SECOND)

DRAINAGE AREA (ACRES)

FIGURE 7.—ESTIMATED **10-YEAR** RATES OF RUNOFF FOR **SLOPING LAND** WITH **LIGHT-
TEXTURED, DEEP, WELL-DRAINED** SOILS IN THE **COASTAL PLAINS** OF **NEW
JERSEY, DELAWARE** AND **MARYLAND**.

30

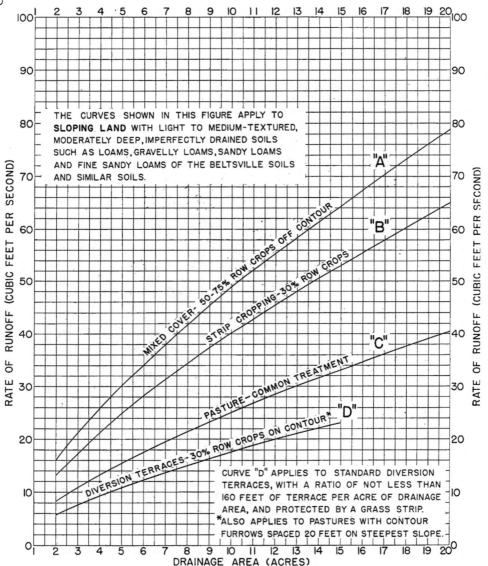

FIGURE 8.-ESTIMATED **IO-YEAR** RATES OF RUNOFF FOR **SLOPING LAND** WITH **MEDIUM
TO LIGHT-TEXTURED, MODERATELY DEEP, IMPERFECTLY DRAINED SOILS** IN THE
COASTAL PLAINS OF **NEW JERSEY, DELAWARE** AND **MARYLAND.**

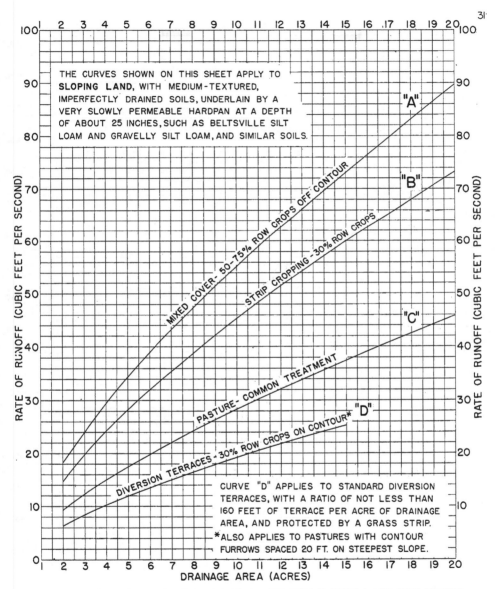

THE CURVES SHOWN ON THIS SHEET APPLY TO SLOPING LAND, WITH MEDIUM-TEXTURED, IMPERFECTLY DRAINED SOILS, UNDERLAIN BY A VERY SLOWLY PERMEABLE HARDPAN AT A DEPTH OF ABOUT 25 INCHES, SUCH AS BELTSVILLE SILT LOAM AND GRAVELLY SILT LOAM, AND SIMILAR SOILS.

"A"

"B"

"C"

"D"

MIXED COVER - 50-75% ROW CROPS OFF CONTOUR

STRIP CROPPING - 30% ROW CROPS

PASTURE - COMMON TREATMENT

DIVERSION TERRACES - 30% ROW CROPS ON CONTOUR*

CURVE "D" APPLIES TO STANDARD DIVERSION TERRACES, WITH A RATIO OF NOT LESS THAN 160 FEET OF TERRACE PER ACRE OF DRAINAGE AREA, AND PROTECTED BY A GRASS STRIP.
*ALSO APPLIES TO PASTURES WITH CONTOUR FURROWS SPACED 20 FT. ON STEEPEST SLOPE.

RATE OF RUNOFF (CUBIC FEET PER SECOND)

DRAINAGE AREA (ACRES)

FIGURE 9.-ESTIMATED 10 YEAR RATES OF RUNOFF FOR SLOPING LAND WITH MEDIUM-TEXTURED, SHALLOW, IMPERFECTLY-DRAINED SOILS IN THE COASTAL PLAINS OF NEW JERSEY, DELAWARE AND MARYLAND.

32

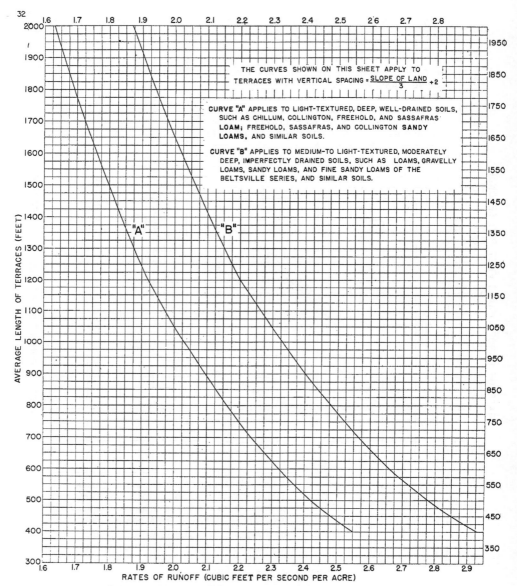

THE CURVES SHOWN ON THIS SHEET APPLY TO
TERRACES WITH VERTICAL SPACING = $\frac{\text{SLOPE OF LAND}}{3}$ +2

CURVE "A" APPLIES TO LIGHT-TEXTURED, DEEP, WELL-DRAINED SOILS,
SUCH AS CHILLUM, COLLINGTON, FREEHOLD, AND SASSAFRAS
LOAM; FREEHOLD, SASSAFRAS, AND COLLINGTON SANDY
LOAMS, AND SIMILAR SOILS.

CURVE "B" APPLIES TO MEDIUM-TO LIGHT-TEXTURED, MODERATELY
DEEP, IMPERFECTLY DRAINED SOILS, SUCH AS LOAMS, GRAVELLY
LOAMS, SANDY LOAMS, AND FINE SANDY LOAMS OF THE
BELTSVILLE SERIES, AND SIMILAR SOILS.

"A"   "B"

AVERAGE LENGTH OF TERRACES (FEET)

RATES OF RUNOFF (CUBIC FEET PER SECOND PER ACRE)

FIGURE 10.—ESTIMATED 10-YEAR RATES OF RUNOFF FROM CROPLAND TERRACES
IN THE COASTAL PLAINS OF NEW JERSEY, DELAWARE, AND MARYLAND.

Discussion of Results

The 10-year curves shown in *figures 2 to 5 and 7 to 10* are based upon very short periods of runoff records (6 yrs. or less). The relative positions of the various curves represent the best values that can be derived from the records at this time. Some of the studies have been discontinued (Freehold) and for this reason the 'A' curves in *figures 2, 3, 4, 8, and 9,* and the 'B' curve in *figure 7* for mixed cover, 50 to 75 percent row crops off-contour, cannot be improved by having longer records become available in the future. The continuance of the College Park studies will assure some longer and consequently more useful records for improving the reliability of some of the curves. Another 3 years of record on W-I will give data on up and down tillage with 30 percent row crops on imperfectly drained soils, while W-II will furnish a better curve for strip cropping on well-drained soils ('E' curve in *fig. 7*) at the end of the same period. The pasture, woodland, and diversion-terrace curves can be based on longer periods of record. The positions of some of the curves will probably be changed somewhat with additional years of record.

The ranges in area shown by the curves are believed to cover ordinary requirements for the Coastal Plains area. Terraced areas exceeding 40 acres would seldom be encountered that would drain into one terrace outlet. Single diversion terraces normally would not have drainage areas exceeding 15 acres. Pastures draining into one drainageway would not be likely to exceed 200 acres; for above this limit mixed cover conditions would prevail. Undisturbed or well-managed woodland would not exceed 40 acres on one drainage area. Cut-over woodland and mixed cover conditions would predominate on areas from 200 to 1,000 acres.

The curves as presented herein are considered to be indicative of the effect of land use and soil conditions on runoff rates. They are believed to have an academic or teaching value to non-technical workers or students who wish to gain better concepts of soil and water conservation and use.

The engineer or technician concerned with the planning of structures or practices on larger drainage areas will find *figures 7 to 10* useful in studying the over-all effects of changed land use on such areas. They should be a material aid in interpolating between curves 'A' and 'B' in *figures 2 to 4*, pages 18 to 20, (for mixed cover and pastures) by evaluating the existing or planned types of land use in terms of the soil conditions that apply in a given case.

FACTORS AFFECTING THE MAGNITUDE OF RUNOFF PEAKS

Examination of the records showed that peak rates of runoff varied considerably from area to area even when the rainfall intensities and amounts were quite similar. The maximum rainfall intensities did not necessarily produce the maximum runoff on a given watershed. Analyses of some of the differences showed them to be due to many factors of which rainfall intensity was only one. A comparison of the peak rates of runoff from some of the experimental areas and analyses of the differences in these rates are included in the following portion of this report.

Surgent, W-I

Rainfall Intensities and Soil Moisture

In the 6 years of record on the Surgent terraced watershed *(figs. 12 and 13, pp. 48 and 49, and pl. 5),* the 10 highest peak rates of runoff were arranged in descending order of magnitude (rank) and compared with the corresponding maximum rainfall intensities for durations of 10, 30, and 60 minutes. The comparisons are shown below:

TABLE 10.--*Peak rates of runoff for the Surgent (W-I) terraced watershed (Freehold, N. J.) and corresponding maximum rates of rainfall.*

Date of storm	Peak rate of runoff		Maximum rainfall rates for durations of					
			10 minutes		30 minutes		60 minutes	
	Inches/hr	Rank	In/hr.	Rank	In/hr.	Rank	In/hr.	Rank
June 30, 1941 (No. 1)	1.77	1	4.32	5	2.82	2	None	
Aug. 19, 1940.	1.76	2	2.58	20	1.96	9	1.42	4
July 15, 1938	1.68	3	4.02	6	1.50	14	None	
June 17, 1943	1.56	4	5.64	1	2.40	3	1.26	6
June 23, 1938	1.33	5	5.58	2	3.36	1	2.09	1
July 8, 1941	1.31	6	2.94	14	1.20	21	.60	25
June 12, 1938	1.28	7	5.22	3	2.14	7	1.14	8
June 26, 1938	1.19	8	2.82	15	1.42	17	.83	15
June 27, 1938	1.16	9	1.92	30	1.24	19	.80	17
June 30, 1941 (No. 2)	1.03	10	3.36	10	1.54	12	1.36	5

A comparison of the storm of June 23, 1938, with that of July 8, 1941, is given below:

June 23, 1938		July 8, 1941	
Peak rate of runoff	— Rank 5	Peak rate of runoff	— Rank 6
10 min. rainfall	— Rank 2	10 min. rainfall	— Rank 14
30 min. rainfall	— Rank 1	30 min. rainfall	— Rank 21
60 min. rainfall	— Rank 1	60 min. rainfall	— Rank 25
9-day antecedent rain	0.12 inch	9-day antecedent rain	6.90 inches

The highest rainfall intensities for 30 and 60 minutes and the second highest for 10 minutes produced a peak rate of runoff on June 23, 1938, that ranked only fifth in order of magnitude. The storm of July 8, 1941, produced a peak rate of runoff that ranked sixth in magnitude. The 10-minute, 30-minute, and 60-minute rainfall intensities, however, ranked only 14, 21, and 25, respectively. Obviously other factors than rainfall intensities determined the magnitude of peak rates of flow. That one of these other factors is the amount of moisture in the soil prior to runoff is evidenced by a comparison of the 9-day antecedent rainfall for the two storms.

W-I vs W-V vs W-X

Where small watersheds are adjacent, or close together, they are generally subject to the same rainfall-intensity patterns and prior rainfalls. If rainfall were the only factor or even the most important factor, a particular rain should produce similar runoffs on such areas, and over a period of years the rank of runoffs should parallel the rainfall ranking. In *table 11* is a listing of the 10 highest runoffs for W-I (8.22 acres, strip cropped) and corresponding runoffs on W-V (4.07 acres, contour planted above a diversion terrace) and corresponding rainfalls for a 6-year period at College Park. The areas are a distance of about 400 feet apart and throughout the period each had about 30 percent row crops (corn or sorghum) planted within 2 percent of the contour. The other crops in the 3-year rotation were hay and winter grain, so that each of the areas had about the same proportion of the three crops each year (refer to *figs. 17 and 18*, pp. 55 and 56, *and pl. 6*, p. 38).

PLATE 5

A. View of cropland terrace T-1 on the H. Surgent farm (W-I) near Freehold, N. J.,
on November 6, 1937. Planting and cultivation of spinach is parallel with terrace
ridge on the right. A Sudan grass cover crop strip lies between spinach and kale
strip on left. The terrace channel drains toward house in background.

B. Method of handling point rows in spinach field where terrace ridges are not parallel. View was taken November 20, 1942, between terraces T-7 and T-8 on the
Surgent farm (see figs. 12 and 13).

38

TABLE 11.--*Peak rates of runoff for College Park, Md., watersheds W-1 (strip cropped) and W-V (contour tillage above terrace) and corresponding maximum rates of rainfall.*

Date of storm	Peak rates of runoff				Maximum rainfall rates for					
	W-I (8.22ac)		W-V (4.07ac)		10 min.		30 min.		60 min.	
	in/hr.	Rank	in/hr.	Rank	in/hr.	Rank	in/hr.	Rank	in/hr.	Rank
July 22, 1945	.3.61	1	1.45	1	6.12	2	3.58	1	none	
Nov. 8, 1943 (No. 1)	1.93	2	.681	3	4.56	6	2.44	4	1.53	1
Aug. 1, 1945	1.91	3	.434	7	4.98	4	2.26	5	1.41	3
July 17, 1945	1.85	4	.656	4	3.24	20	1.86	12	1.20	8
Nov. 8, 1943 (No. 2)	1.80	5	1.13	2	2.76	25	1.82	14	1.28	5
Oct. 15, 1942	1.75	6	.526	6	2.88	24	1.92	10	1.26	6
Aug. 10, 1942	1.67	7	.539	5	5.58	3	2.68	2	none	
June 21, 1945	1.28	8	.383	8	4.20	7	1.98	8	1.35	4
July 26, 1945	1.05	9	.280	10	3.96	11	2.02	7	1.45	2
May 28, 1945	.937	10	.170	17	3.84	12	2.62	3	none	
Average (10) rates	1.78		0.625		(W-V rates 35% of W-I)					
Adjusted for size	[1]2.22		.625		(W-V rates 28% of W-I)					

[1]W-I rates multiplied by area factor (1.245) to bring them to 4.07-acre values for comparison with W-V.

Rainfall Intensities and Soil Moisture

Table 11 indicates, for the College Park watersheds, W-I and W-V, a better agreement between the highest intensities of rainfall and the higher rates of runoff than was the case for the Surgent (W-I) watershed. The three highest rates of runoff on W-I were all produced by storms having relatively high intensities for the 10-minute, 30-minute, and 60-minute periods. However, runoffs of rank four, five, and six on W-I and four, two, and six on W-V were all produced by low intensity storms. As in the July 8, 1941, storm on Surgent W-I, these storms occurred when the soil had been saturated by antecedent rains.

Type of Cover and Its Location with Respect to Gaging Station

For the 6-year period, a comparison of the time of occurrence of peak rates was made for concurrent runoffs from W-I and W-V, when the soil profiles were near saturation. The results of these comparisons are shown in tabular form on the next page:

W-I	W-V
(8.22 acres - Strip cropped within 2% of the contour.)	(4.07 acres - Planted within 2% of the contour above diversion terrace.)
Winter Seasons	
Complete coverage - wheat, hay, and rough plowed.	Complete coverage - wheat, hay, and rough plowed.
	Peaks occured 4 minutes to 3 hours later than those on W-I.
Summer Seasons	
1940 and 1943 - Row-crop strips closest to gaging station.	1940 and 1943 - Row-crop field farthest from gaging station.
	Peaks occurred 3 to 43 minutes later than those on W-I.
1941 and 1944 - Row-crop strips in intermediate position.	1941 and 1944 - Row-crop field in middle of area.
	Peaks occurred from 15 to 35 minutes later than those on W-I.
Summer Seasons	
1942 and 1945 - Row-crop strips farthest from gaging station.	1942 and 1945 - Row-crop field closest to gaging station.
Peaks occurred from 0 to 15 minutes later than those on W-V.	

In the winter seasons, disregarding runoffs where snow distribution was uneven or the melting of snow was unequal due to differences in exposure, the peaks from the diversion terrace on W-V generally occurred from 4 minutes to 2 to 3 hours later than those on W-I. In the summer seasons, when the cultivated area was in the middle field or the south field of W-V, the runoffs generally lagged from 3 to 43 minutes behind those of W-I. In 1942 and 1945, when the row crop was nearest the runoff station on W-V (northern field) and most remote on W-I, the peak occurred on W-V either at the same instant or earlier by 5 to 15 minutes than that on W-I. From the foregoing, two deductions may be made: (1) That the cultivated land produces the greatest proportion of runoff, even though contour planted, in comparison with the grain and hay fields, and (2) that the location of the cultivated fields or strips determine the period of rise of the hydrographs and influence the magnitude of the peaks.

Channel Storage.--Samples of runoff water have always shown considerably lower concentrations of silt on W-V than on W-I. This is evidence of the degree of velocity control in the channels removing the runoff. The diversion-channel grade of 0.44 foot per hundred feet on W-V controls the speed more effectively than the average grade of 3 feet per hundred feet on W-I. The actual values of the runoff peaks are shown in table 11. A comparison of some important factors including the average of the 10 highest peaks on W-I with the corresponding peaks on W-V is shown below:

W-I	W-V
(8.22 acres - Strip cropped.)	(4.07 acres - Contour planted above a diversion terrace.)
Average slope of waterway = 3 feet per 100 feet.	Diversion-terrace grade = 0.44 foot per 100 feet.
	Silt concentration in runoff water less than for W-I.
Average 10 highest peaks = 1.78 inches per hour.	Average 10 corresponding peaks = 0.625 inch per hour.
Average corrected to 4.07 acres = 2.22 inches per hour.	0.625 inch per hour.

PLATE 6

A, Panorama of strip-cropped areas near College Park on Nov. 15, 1939, at start of initial comparative period, looking southeast. A 3-year rotation of corn, grain, and hay was being followed. The dividing dike in the center forms areas W-I (left) and W-II (right). The corn was shocked in center of nearest strips and on both edges of farthest strips. Winter barley was coming up on the corn strips. Instrument shelter and gaging stations are next to woods beyond most distant shocks. W-V lies above corn shocks on extreme right.

B, View of water standing between corn stubble rows on W-I after 0.76 inch rain in 8 hours on Sept. 25, 1940. This storm produced negligible runoff at the station, and the water had percolated into the soil 80 minutes later. Corn stubble had not been disked for winter barley yet.

C, Silt and sand 10 inches deep accumulated at lower end of the middle field on W-II on June 7, 1945, from corn planted up and down the slope. Wash occurred in every planter mark and some of the 4 inch corn plants were completely washed out. Caused by rains of 1.61 inches on May 28 and 1.33 inches on June 2, with 10-minute intensities of 3.8 and 3.2 inches per hour, respectively.

The 10 highest peaks on W-I average 1.78 inches per hour while the corresponding peaks on W-V average 0.625 inch per hour. The W-V rates average but 35 percent of those on W-I. Multiplying the W-I rates by the area factor of 1.245 taken from the area-factor curves already discussed, brings W-I rates to the values that can be expected from a strip-cropped drainage area of 4.07 acres, the same size as W-V. On this basis, the average rates on W-I are increased to 2.22 inches per hour. The W-V rates then average but 28 percent of those on W-I. The low comparative rates on W-V are partly the result of the channel-storage factor in the diversion terrace, which has a marked effect in reducing the magnitude of the peak rates by delaying and leveling off the hydrographs.

Depth and Permeability of Soil

The effect of depth and permeability of soil on the magnitude of peak rates of runoff is shown by the following comparison of the average of the eight highest peaks for 2.4 years from W-I, and the corresponding peaks on W-X and W-V:

W-I	W-X	W-V
(8.22 acres — Strip cropped.)	(3.04 acres— Strip cropped above a diversion terrace.)	(4.07 acres — Contour planted above a diversion terrace.)
Moderately deep soil.	Shallow to moderately deep	Moderately deep soil.
10% well-drained	38% well-drained	100% well-drained
Average of 8 highest peaks corrected to 4.07 acres = 100% of W-I average.	Average of 8 corresponding peaks corrected to 4.07 acres = 34% of W-I average.	Average of 8 corresponding peaks = 29% of W-I average.

The Chillum loam and gravelly loam on W-V are moderately deep and 100 percent well-drained, whereas the Beltsville and Leonardtown loams and Berwyn silt loam on W-I, while also classed as moderately deep, are somewhat shallower than on W-V and 90 percent imperfectly drained. W-X, a nearby 3.04-acre area above a diversion terrace, strip cropped nearer to the contour than W-I or W-V (see figs. 17 and 18, pp. 55 and 56) has soils that are shallow to moderately deep and 62 percent imperfectly drained. It is, therefore, intermediate between W-I and W-V in drainage condition. It has a short record of runoff of only 2.4 years, but comparison of the peak rates of the eight highest runoffs on W-I (adjusted to 4.07 acres) for this short period with the corresponding rates on W-X (also adjusted to 4.07 acres) and W-V actual rates, shows that W-V rates average 29 percent and W-X rates average 34 percent of those on W-I. It seems reasonable to assume that the relatively low peaks on W-V were due in part to the moderately deep, well-drained soils on that area.

W-III vs W-IV

Direction of Tillage

Direction of tillage may overshadow the effect of all other factors on the magnitude of peak runoff rates. This was found to be true in the following comparison of peak rates from adjacent areas W-III and W-IV:

W—III	W—IV
Area = 6.06 acres Truck crops. 94% deep well—drained soil	Area = 6.11 acres Truck crops. 54% deep well—drained soil
1942	
Up and downhill tillage Average of 5 corresponding peaks = 100%	Contour tillage Average of 5 highest peaks = 19% of that for W—III
1943 and 1944	
Contour tillage Average of 5 corresponding peaks = 37% of that for W—IV.	Up and downhill tillage Average of 5 highest peaks = 100%

Areas W-III and W-IV were practically equal in size (6.06 and 6.11 acres) and were both devoted to the production of truck crops of sweet corn, baby lima beans, and edible soybeans for the 3 years 1942 to 1944 (*see fig. 20*, p. 58). *Figure 19*, page 57, shows that W-III is largely (94 percent) deep and well-drained sandy loam and loam, while 54 percent of W-IV is deep, well-drained loam, and the remaining 46 percent is deep loam and silt loam tending toward imperfect drainage in the lower profile. In 1942, when W-IV was in contour-tilled row crops, the five highest runoffs (0.622, 0.615, 0.138, 0.135, and 0.111 in./hr.) averaged 19 percent of the concurrent peaks on W-III (1.36, 3.17, 1.10, 1.88, and 1.22 in./hr., respectively), tilled up and down the slope. In 1943 (*pl. 7*) and 1944, when the direction of tillage was reversed on the two watersheds, the five peaks (0.656, 1.87, 1.29, 0.626, and 0.437 in./hr.) on contour-tilled W-III averaged only 37 percent of the corresponding five highest flows (4.33, 2.97, 2.24, 2.21, and 1.37 in./hr., respectively) on W-IV, which was cultivated up and down. Although the differences in the percentages of deep, well-drained soil on the two areas undoubtedly affected the magnitude of the peak runoff rates, the direction of tillage was the predominant factor.

Depth and Permeability of Soil

A comparison of peak rates from the same areas (W-III and W-IV) was made for the period when both areas were in pasture. The results of this comparison are given in the following tabulation:

W—III	W—IV
Area = 5.66 acres Pasture Deep well—drained soil 94% Average of 5 corresponding peaks = 59% of that for W—IV.	Area = 8.01 acres Pasture Deep well—drained soil 54% Average[1] of 5 highest peaks = 100%

[1]Corrected to 5.66 acre-area.

When both areas were in pasture, the five corresponding actual peaks on W-III (5.66 acres) averaged 66 percent of the five highest peaks on W-IV (8.01 acres) or considering size relationships, these peaks were 59 percent of those on W-IV (rates for 5.66 acres). This would indicate that the depth and permeability of the soil may be the dominating factors when the areas are under pasture or when the tillage-direction factor is eliminated.

PLATE 7

A, Lima bean fields on July 16, 1943, near College Park. W-IV planted up and down the slope to the left of the auto, which stands on the dividing dike of the twin areas. W-III (to right) is planted on the contour following two contour base lines. Latest planting is nearest auto.

B, Cultivating lower contour planted strip on W-III on July 16, 1943. Point rows meet lower base line at upper right.

A, Southeast view of pastured watersheds (College Park) on May 29, 1942, in initial period before any furrows were plowed in. Hereford steers are on W-VII beyond 4x4-foot pasture cage used for determining yields. W-VI watershed is in the right background beyond rain gage R-4 on dividing dike.

B, View of furrows on W-VII looking west on May 12, 1943. Three to five inches of water standing in center furrow came from a 1.80-inch rain in 13 hours ending 3.5 hours before. There was negligible runoff on the furrowed pasture W-VII whereas there were three small runoffs on W-VI, the uncontrolled pasture, with a total loss of 0.15 inch of runoff.

W-VI vs W-VII

Depth and Permeability of Soil

The importance of depth and permeability of soil as factors affecting the magnitude of peak rates of runoff is further illustrated by the following comparison of the peak rates from W-VI and W-VII for the initial comparative period:

W-VI	W-VII
Initial 2.7-year Comparative Period	
Common pasture	Common pasture
Moderately deep, soil 48% well-drained	Shallow soil, 100% imperfectly drained
Average of 10 highest peaks = 74% of that for W-VII.	Average of 10 corresponding peaks = 100%

Areas W-VI and W-VII, (*fig. 21*, p. 59, and *pl. 8, A*, p. 42) are adjacent pastured areas. The soils of W-VI are moderately deep, roughly one-half imperfectly drained silt loams, and one-half well-drained sandy loam. The soils of W-VII are predominantly silt loams, shallow, and imperfectly drained. In the first comparative period of 2.7 years, the 10 highest peaks on W-VI (better drained) averaged 74 percent of the corresponding peaks on W-VII (imperfectly drained). On both areas the peaks occurred at about the same time, but varied 5 to 10 minutes on occasion.

Depression Storage

The introduction of an additional factor may at times offset the effect of depth and permeability of soil. This was demonstrated in the comparison of the peak rates of W-III and W-IV where the direction of tillage was shown to be the predominant factor. A further illustration is provided in the following comparison of peak rates from W-VI and W-VII for the second comparative period:

W-VI	W-VII
Moderately deep soil	Shallow soil
48% well-drained	100% imperfectly drained
Initial 2.7-year Comparative Period	
Common pasture	Common pasture
Average of 10 highest peaks = 74% of that for W-VII.	Average of 10 corresponding peaks = 100%
Second 2.6-year Comparative Period	
Common pasture	Pasture with 20-foot contour furrows
Average of 10 corresponding peaks = 100%	Average of 10 highest peaks = 75% of that for W-VI.

During the second period of 2.6 years, after the 20-foot contour furrows had been added to W-VII (*pl. 8, B*), the 10 highest peaks averaged 75 percent of the 10 corresponding peaks on W-VII or a net reduction on W-VII of 44 percent in magnitude. The time of peaks on W-VII generally lagged 3 to 15 minutes behind W-VI. Creation of depression storage on W-VII by the construction of the furrows greatly reduced and delayed the runoff peaks on the shallow, relatively tight soil.

Contour Furrows vs Common Pasture

Peak rates of runoff from W-VI, above a low minimum limit were plotted against corresponding values from W-VII for both first and second comparative periods. These plottings resulted in considerable scatter, as shown in the two upper diagrams in *figure 11*, even though the areas were in pasture. Rather than determine a regression line for this scatter of concurrent peaks, the data for each watershed for each of the two periods were evaluated on a frequency of recurrence basis. Peak rates for various frequencies

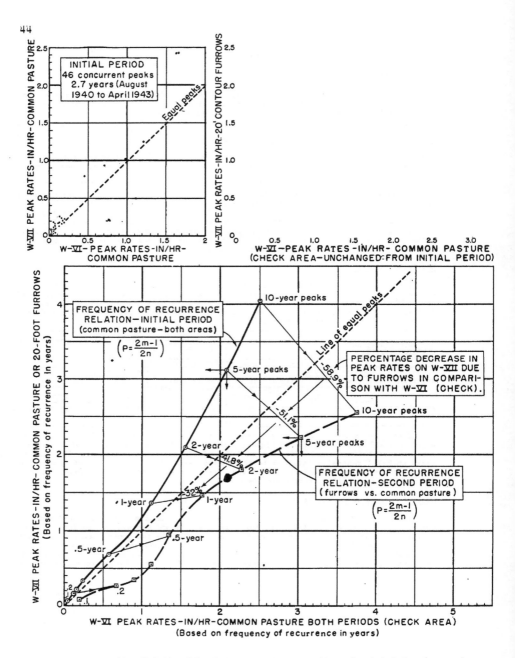

FIGURE 11.--Relationships between pasture practices for initial and second periods W-VI and W-VII, College Park, Md.

for W-VI were then plotted against the corresponding values for W-VII for both initial
and second comparative periods *(lower diagram, fig. 11)*. For 2-year peaks in the initial
period the W-VII values were 135.5 percent of those on W-VI $(2.10 \times 100/1.55)$. In the
second period, with furrows on W-VII, 2-year peaks were 78.9 percent of those on W-VI
which was unchanged $(1.80 \times 100/2.28)$. Using W-VI as a check area the net change on
W-VII due to placing of the furrows was $100 - (78.9 \times 100/135.5)$ or 41.8 percent de-
crease in peak rates. Values or relationships derived indirectly by the methods described above have their limitations in use but are of considerable aid to judgment. It
is believed that ratios of peak frequencies for a recurrence interval of about the length
of the comparative periods are safer to use in determining such relationships than higher
values, such as 5 or 10-year peaks which are based upon extrapolations of the curves.

W-VIII vs W-IX

Woodland Litter

The effect of woodland litter upon the magnitude and time of occurrence of peak
rates of runoff is shown in the following comparison of peak rates from W-VIII with those
from W-IX.

W-VIII	W-IX
Area = 2.43 acres	Area = 12.05 acres
Moderately deep soil, imperfectly drained	Moderately deep soil, well-drained
Cut-over woodland	Mature woodland
Good to poor litter	Uniformly good litter
Average of 6 highest peaks = 100%	Average[1] of 6 corresponding peaks = 22% of that of W-VIII
	Peaks occurred from 15 minutes to 2 hours later than those on W-VIII.

[1]Corrected to 2.43 acres.

The wooded watersheds at College Park are 0.8 of a mile apart and both have moderately deep soils. Area W-IX consists of 12.05 acres of mature woodland and is well-
drained. Area W-VIII consists of 2.43 acres of cut-over woodland and is imperfectly
drained. The six actual peaks for W-IX, in 5 years, compared with the corresponding six
highest peaks on W-VIII average 13 percent of those for the cut-over area. Increasing
W-IX rates to 2.43 acres by multiplying by the size factor 1.65 shows the six peaks on
W-IX to be 22 percent of those on W-VIII. Field observations indicate that on these
woodlands, where there is a good litter on the forest floor, the rain percolates into the
ground and part of it appears later as subsurface flow. Where the litter is poor or ab-
sent, as on parts of W-VIII *(see pl. 4, A, p. 22)*, some water flows off as surface runoff.
It was also observed that W-IX always reached its peak 15 minutes to 2 hours later than
the smaller area, which would indicate that more subsurface flow takes place on this
watershed than on W-VIII.

DETAILED DESCRIPTIONS OF THE EXPERIMENTAL AREAS

The characteristics of the 14 watersheds have been summarized in *tables 1 and 2*, pages 4 and 5. The information given in these tables may be sufficient for the casual reader. For those wishing to make a more comprehensive study of the results presented in this publication, descriptions in greater detail are given in the following pages. It is anticipated that the results of the analysis of total runoff from the areas will be added to the report at a later date. When this is done, the revised and enlarged publication will constitute a complete summary of the studies. To further this objective, the maps, cropping histories, and all other information pertinent to the areas should be available to the reader. Such descriptions will be found in the following paragraphs and in the maps on pages 48 to 52 and 55 to 60.

Freehold Watersheds

The areas near Freehold, N. J., were selected on private farms lying within the former 17,133-acre Manalapan Creek Demonstration Project of the Soil Conservation Service in Monmouth County. This is now a part of the official Soil Conservation District NJ-3. The four watersheds lie near the headwaters of Manalapan Creek, a tributary of the Raritan River.

W-I lies on the farm of H. Surgent, 1-3/4 miles southwest of Freehold, N. J. The soils are deep and well-drained. Freehold sandy loam occupies 91 percent of the area, and Collington loam the remaining 9 percent. Erosion had been severe on 65 percent of the area as indicated in erosion map, *figure 12*. For a number of years the area within the watershed line had produced truck crops such as lima beans, spinach, onions, chicory, kale, broccoli, cucumbers, etc. Rows were run up and down the 1 to 12 percent slope, parallel with the main county highway to Freehold. In 1937, nine broad-base cropland terraces were constructed on the area, as shown on the topographic map, *figure 12*, page 48. These discharged into a previously vegetated terrace-outlet channel 16 feet wide, running up the central part of the area. This channel was designed for a flow of 60 cubic feet per second. On August 17, 1938, terraces T-8 and T-9 *(fig. 13)* were extended to the east, increasing the drainage area from 15.7 to 17.5 acres. Data on terrace lengths, channel slopes, and actual vertical intervals of the terraces compared with those recommended for the Northeastern States by the Soil Conservation Service are also given in *figure 13*, together with some typical cross sections. The height of the terraces was fairly well maintained by plowing to the ridges. Truck crops were planted on the terraces parallel with the terrace ridge and on the approximate contour, with the point rows generally coming between the terraces as illustrated in *plate 5*, page 35. The kind of crops, the lay-out of rows, etc., are shown in *figure 12* for 1941. When possible, Surgent planted Sudan grass between short season crops, and plowed it under for green manure. He also applied barnyard manure on the land about every 2 years. The land generally had no winter cover except some crop residues and weeds.

W-II on the T. Smith farm lies 3.5 miles southwest of Freehold, N. J., and 1 mile south of Millhurst, N. J., *(see fig. 14)*. It originally had a natural watershed area of 34.2 acres which was reduced to 32.9 acres in February 1939 by placing a channel into the woods on the northeast margin of the drainage area. Freehold sandy loam comprises 87 percent of the area, with 12 percent of Collington loam which is also deep and well-drained. There has been considerable deposition of soil from the higher lying slopes in the main drainageway as shown in the erosion map, *figure 14*. This deposit absorbs small runoffs completely and reduces the medium flows to a considerable degree. The land has been devoted to rather intensive use in the production of potatoes and general crops during the growing seasons, but all areas were protected by a winter cover crop of rye. Field 2a had an annual crop of corn except in 1939 when it had hay and cowpeas. Field 2b had a 2-year rotation in corn and hay, or corn and soybeans. Both fields were planted off-contour, as shown in *figure 14*. Field 3 was strip cropped on the contour in 1939, and the diversion terrace was added in August 1940. The strips were cropped with wheat and soybeans or corn, wheat, hay, and alfalfa. Field 4 produced soybeans for 4 years and corn for 2 years. Fields 5 and 6 were planted off the contour to potatoes every year. Field 7 had soybeans and corn alternating and was contour planted.

W-III is located 0.4 mile southwest of W-I or about 2 miles from Freehold, mainly on the T. Sherrard farm. *(See fig. 15.)* Parts of three other farms comprise the remainder of the natural watershed area, totaling 51.8 acres. Freehold loam and sandy loam occupy 84 percent of the area and are deep and well-drained. The Shrewsbury loam and sandy loam and the Adelphia sandy loam occupy the remaining 16 percent of the area and are deep, imperfectly to poorly drained. They lie principally along the main drainage channel, and about two-thirds are accumulations from areas above. Unlike W-I and W-II, this watershed had continuous runoff for the period of record. Fields 1, 2, 4, and 5 were in permanent pasture, comprising 22 percent of the area. Field 3 produced potatoes on off-contour planting every year except 1941 and 1942 when soybeans and oats were planted and pastured. Field 6 was planted to potatoes off-contour in 1939, 1941, and 1943, with rye and hay in alternating years. Fields 7 and 13 were used for garden truck and strawberries. Field 8 was idle with a cover of grass, weeds, and brush. Fields 9a and 9b were in alfalfa every year, except in 1940 when potatoes were harvested from both, and in 1939 when field 9a also produced a crop of potatoes. Fields 10 and 12 produced potatoes every year. Field 11 was in hay or alfalfa all of the period. In most cases, the potato fields were protected with a rye winter cover crop. A 24-inch culvert under the farm road between fields 2 and 4 caused backing up of the higher flows. This tended to reduce the peaks recorded at the gaging station. Pondage corrections consequently were made to the hydrographs of the larger storms to eliminate the effect of restricted flow through this culvert.

W-IV is a drainage area of 102.7 acres lying principally on the William Ward and G. J. Johnson farms, 6 miles southwest of Freehold and 2 miles from Millhurst. Ninety-three percent of the area was mapped as Freehold sandy loam and loamy sand, as shown in *figure 16*, page 52, and is classed as deep, well to excessively drained. Considerable deposition of eroded materials has taken place along the drainageways representing about 10 percent of the watershed. The upper two-thirds of this area is excessively drained loamy sand and probably reduces peak rates somewhat. The lower third of the deposits, just above the gaging station, is poorly drained. The watershed produced runoff almost continuously for the first 15 months when the precipitation was normal or above. In June 1939, a drainage channel was constructed for 450 feet above the weir, and tile was placed up to 862 feet in order to drain the poorly drained area described above. This did not adequately solve the problem, so in November 1939 nineteen 2-inch drain holes were drilled through the base of the concrete weir to lower the water table. From this time onward, no base flow could be recorded, and only the intermittent surface runoffs were obtained. However, the effect on the high rates of runoff utilized in this publication is considered negligible. The rate of flow through the drain holes was of the order of a small fraction of a cubic foot per second, while the lowest rates of runoff used in determining the frequency of recurrence of peak rates were of the order of 10 cubic feet per second. Off-contour cropping of the areas was followed during the period of record. The lower maps in *figure 16* show the crops in June 1938 and May 1940. In other years, the cropping was quite similar.

48

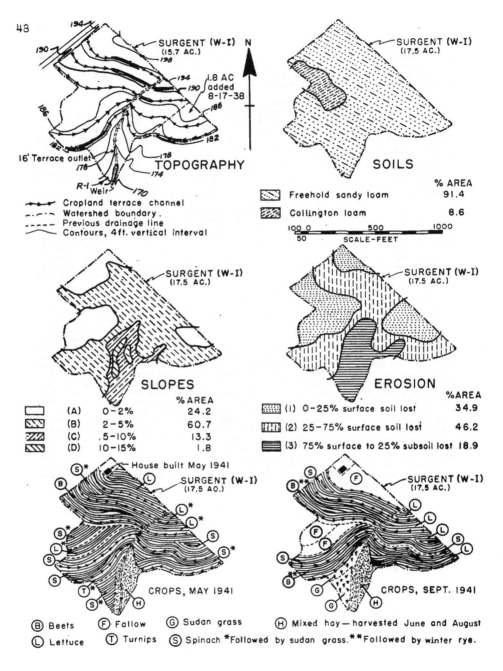

SURGENT (W-I)
(15.7 AC.)

1.8 AC
added
8-17-38

16' Terrace outlet

R-I Weir

TOPOGRAPHY

→→→→ Cropland terrace channel
-..-..- Watershed boundary.
------ Previous drainage line
⌒⌒⌒ Contours, 4ft. vertical interval

SURGENT (W-I)
(17.5 AC.)

SOILS

                              % AREA
▨ Freehold sandy loam   91.4
▨ Collington loam   8.6

100 0   500   1000
  50   SCALE-FEET

SURGENT (W-I)
(17.5 AC.)

SLOPES

                %AREA
☐ (A) 0-2%   24.2
▨ (B) 2-5%   60.7
▨ (C) 5-10%   13.3
▨ (D) 10-15%   1.8

SURGENT (W-I)
(17.5 AC.)

EROSION

                                        %AREA
▨ (1) 0-25% surface soil lost   34.9
▨ (2) 25-75% surface soil lost   46.2
▨ (3) 75% surface to 25% subsoil lost   18.9

House built May 1941

SURGENT (W-I)
(17.5 AC.)

CROPS, MAY 1941

SURGENT (W-I)
(17.5 AC.)

CROPS, SEPT. 1941

Ⓑ Beets   Ⓕ Fallow   Ⓖ Sudan grass   Ⓗ Mixed hay—harvested June and August
Ⓛ Lettuce   Ⓣ Turnips   Ⓢ Spinach *Followed by sudan grass.**Followed by winter rye.

FIGURE 12.--Physiographic characteristics and typical cropping procedures on the
cropland terraces of the H. Surgent farm (W-I) near Freehold, N. J.

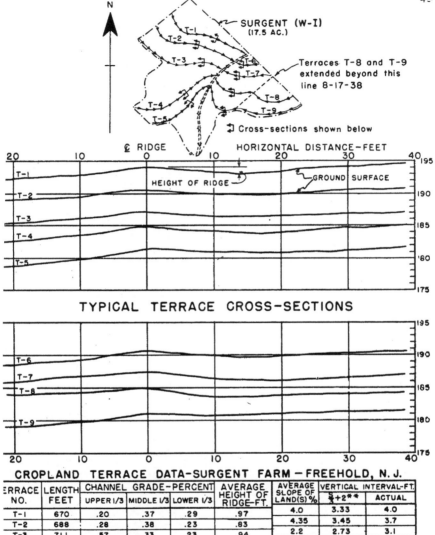

TYPICAL TERRACE CROSS-SECTIONS

CROPLAND TERRACE DATA-SURGENT FARM — FREEHOLD, N.J.

TERRACE NO.	LENGTH FEET	CHANNEL GRADE-PERCENT			AVERAGE HEIGHT OF RIDGE-FT.	AVERAGE SLOPE OF LAND(S) %	VERTICAL INTERVAL-FT.	
		UPPER 1/3	MIDDLE 1/3	LOWER 1/3			$\frac{S}{4}+2$**	ACTUAL
T-1	670	.20	.37	.29	.97	4.0	3.33	4.0
T-2	688	.28	.38	.23	.83	4.35	3.45	3.7
T-3	711	.57	.33	.23	.94	2.2	2.73	3.1
T-4	692	.03	.42	.43	1.09	1.7	2.57	3.0
T-5	610	.32	.26	.49	.88	3.15	3.05	2.4
T-6	165	.18	.30	1.75*	.58	3.75	3.25	3.0
T-7	362	1.10*	.12	.25	.92	3.45	3.15	3.4
T-8	650	.45	.44	.41	.93	1.75	2.58	2.5
T-9	850	.14	.50	.34	.58	2.15	2.72	2.9
AVERAGE	600	.27	.34	.33	.87	2.95	2.98	3.1

Based on field survey of May 30, 1944.   *Not included in averages.   **N.E. Region Specifications.

13.--Cropland terrace lay-out and typical cross sections after 7 years of use on the H. Surgent farm (W-I) near Freehold, N. J.

50

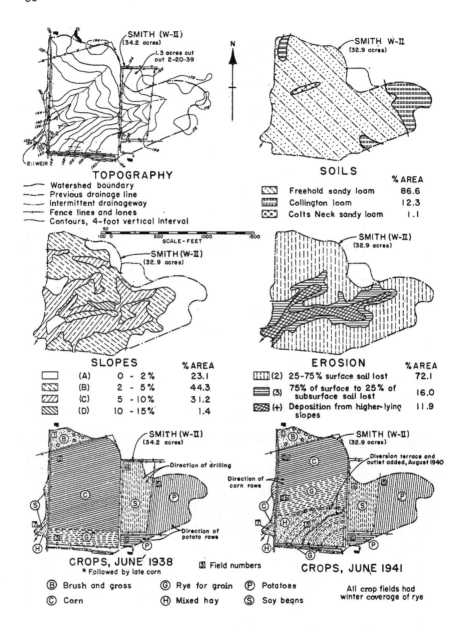

TOPOGRAPHY

— · — Watershed boundary
— · · — Previous drainage line
— · · · — Intermittent drainageway
— · — Fence lines and lanes
——— Contours, 4-foot vertical interval

SOILS

		% AREA
	Freehold sandy loam	86.6
	Collington loam	12.3
	Colts Neck sandy loam	1.1

SLOPES

		% AREA
(A)	0 - 2%	23.1
(B)	2 - 5%	44.3
(C)	5 - 10%	31.2
(D)	10 - 15%	1.4

EROSION

		% AREA
(2)	25-75% surface soil lost	72.1
(3)	75% of surface to 25% of subsurface soil lost	16.0
(+)	Deposition from higher-lying slopes	11.9

CROPS, JUNE 1938
* Followed by late corn

⬚ Field numbers

Ⓑ Brush and grass
Ⓒ Corn
Ⓖ Rye for grain
Ⓗ Mixed hay
Ⓟ Potatoes
Ⓢ Soy beans

CROPS, JUNE 1941

All crop fields had winter coverage of rye

FIGURE 14.- Physiographic characteristics and typical cropping plan on the T. Smith (W-Ⅱ) watershed near Freehold, N. J.

51

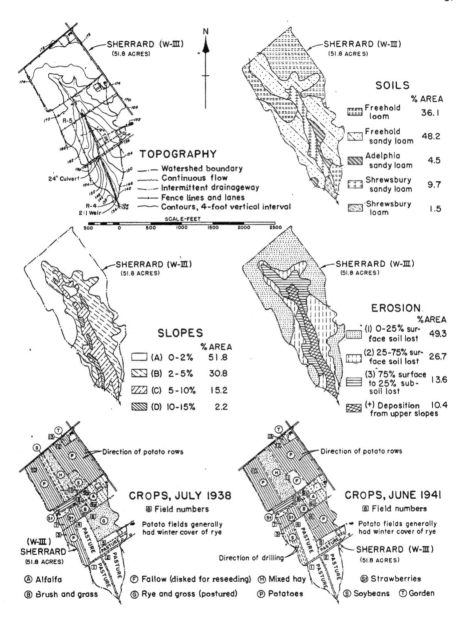

SHERRARD (W-Ⅲ)
(51.8 ACRES)

N

TOPOGRAPHY
-..- Watershed boundary
——— Continuous flow
-·-·- Intermittent drainageway
-··-··- Fence lines and lanes
——— Contours, 4-foot vertical interval

24" Culvert

R-5

R-4
2:1 Weir

SCALE-FEET
500   0   500   1000   1500   2000   2500

SHERRARD (W-Ⅲ)
(51.8 ACRES)

SOILS
                              % AREA
Freehold loam   36.1
Freehold sandy loam   48.2
Adelphia sandy loam   4.5
Shrewsbury sandy loam   9.7
Shrewsbury loam   1.5

SHERRARD (W-Ⅲ)
(51.8 ACRES)

SLOPES
                    % AREA
(A) 0-2%   51.8
(B) 2-5%   30.8
(C) 5-10%   15.2
(D) 10-15%   2.2

SHERRARD (W-Ⅲ)
(51.8 ACRES)

EROSION
                              % AREA
(I) 0-25% sur-face soil lost 49.3
(2) 25-75% sur-face soil lost 26.7
(3) 75% surface to 25% sub-soil lost 13.6
(+) Deposition from upper slopes 10.4

Direction of potato rows

CROPS, JULY 1938
Ⓑ Field numbers
Potato fields generally had winter cover of rye

(W-Ⅲ)
SHERRARD
(51.8 ACRES)

PASTURE

Ⓐ Alfalfa
Ⓑ Brush and grass

Ⓕ Fallow (disked for reseeding)
Ⓖ Rye and grass (pastured)

Direction of potato rows

CROPS, JUNE 1941
Ⓑ Field numbers
Potato fields generally had winter cover of rye

SHERRARD (W-Ⅲ)
(51.8 ACRES)

Direction of drilling

PASTURE

Ⓗ Mixed hay
Ⓟ Potatoes

Ⓢⓣ Strawberries
Ⓢ Soybeans   Ⓣ Garden

FIGURE 15.—Physiographic characteristics and typical cropping plan for the J. Sherrard (W-Ⅲ) watershed near Freehold, N.J.

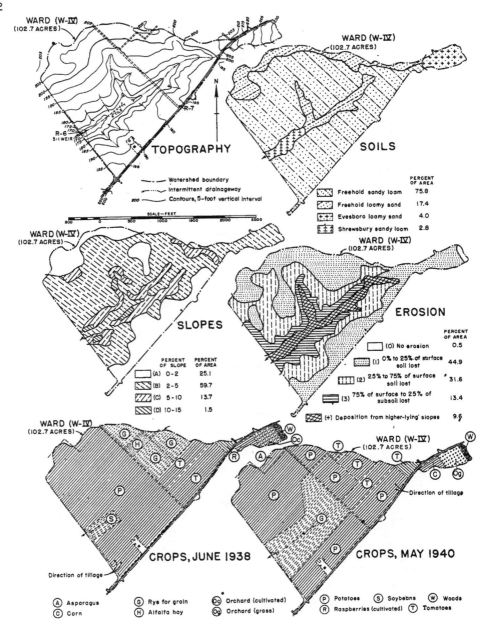

FIGURE 16.—Physiographic characteristics and typical planting lay-out on the W. Ward (W-IV) drainage area near Freehold, N. J.

College Park Watersheds

The College Park, Md., areas, located about 7 miles north-northwest of the University of Maryland campus, lie within the drainage area of the Little Paint Branch, except W-IX which is on Paint Branch. Both branches are a part of the Anacostia River system. All areas are located within a circle, 1.2 miles in diameter.

W-I, W-II, W-V, and W-X all lie within an original drainage area of about 35 acres which had been farmed many years in large rectangular fields, mostly off-contour. In 1938, a hedgerow was removed and replaced by a vegetated terrace-outlet channel. Four diversion terraces were constructed to drain into this outlet which conveyed the runoff water across the road to the east and spread it out in the woods as shown in the maps, *figures 17 and 18.* A fifth diversion terrace was constructed below the two on the western slope and discharged runoff into the woods on the south. This system of water disposal protected the lower 15.7-acre field from runoff from the higher lying slopes. This lower area was strip cropped in 1939 in uniform strips of 96-foot width following a base line on about the 312 contour. *(See pl. 6, A, p. 38.)* A 3-year rotation of corn, grain, and hay was established on the strips, in the order named, down the slope. *(Refer to fig. 18.)* In June 1939, a dividing dike was constructed up the center of the area forming twin (adjacent) watersheds, W-I of 8.22 acres in the eastern portion, and W-II of 7.44 acres in the western part. W-I was made larger because it was anticipated that the Montgomery County highway would be re-alined with a flatter curve in the road above the 320 contour. This eventuality did not develop, however, and the watersheds remained unequal in area. After a complete rotation in strip cropping (3-yr. initial comparative period) on W-I and W-II, the latter was changed in November 1942 to up and downhill cultivation in three fields planted to the same rotation, while W-I was continued in strip cropping without change. Corn strips or fields for the next year were generally plowed in December and went through the winter in a rough-plowed condition (1940, 1941, 1942, and 1944 crop yrs.). In 1943 and 1945, the plowing was not accomplished until February and March. It is believed that the winter rates of runoff were little affected by the plowing in contrast to sod. In both cases, the most of the rain or melting snows percolated into the sod or plowed ground and became subsurface flow. The corn was planted in May, cut and shocked in September, and the corn stubble disked down and drilled to winter grain in October. In following this cropping procedure, a given field or strip was only exposed to the intense summer rains from May to October, 1 year out of 3. The period when it was in corn or disked for winter grain is actually only about 17 percent of the total time. *(See pl. 6, p. 38, for views of the areas.)*

Records on W-V (4.07 acres) were begun late in 1939 by installing an H-3 flume at the outlet of the 1,000-foot diversion terrace. The dike, channel, and 20-foot filter strip of this terrace are maintained in hay cover. The channel grade averages 0.6 percent for the lower 200 feet and 0.4 percent for the upper 800 feet. The cropland above the vegetated channel was divided into three equal areas and planted on the contour to the same rotation as W-I and W-II, as shown in *figure 18.* In this case, the opportunity for absorption of runoff from the cultivated field, in grain or hay strips below, is lacking. The ground for corn or sorghum was generally plowed in the spring in March or April (1940, 1943, and 1945). In 1944, it was not plowed for sorghum until June 2. In crop years 1941 and 1942, it was plowed in the previous December.

W-X (3.04 acres) was installed in July 1943, by constructing a gaging station similar to W-V at the outlet of the lower diversion terrace on the northerly slope. This channel has a grade of 0.9 percent throughout its 600 feet of length. Beginning in 1944, the area above the 20-foot grass filter strip along the diversion channel was planted to a 3-year rotation of sorghum, wheat, and hay on three contour strips. Each strip-boundary was located on the exact contour. The strips for sorghum were plowed in May 1944 and in March 1945.

The distribution of the soils, slopes, and erosion classes on the four preceding watersheds is shown in *figure 17,* together with the percentages of each. *Table 2,* page 5, gives additional characteristics of the area.

Watersheds W-III and W-IV were located on soils adapted to truck crops. The watersheds were laid out adjacent to each other in the same manner as W-I and W-II. The areas were maintained in ordinary pasture for the first 18 months to provide an initial comparative period to get the differences in runoff characteristics of the areas. W-IV originally had a drainage area of about 10.8 acres, but was reduced to 8.01 acres before runoff measurements started by constructing the upper diversion terrace on the west slope shown on topographic map, figure 19. It was later (April 1941) reduced to 6.11 acres by constructing a second terrace below the first. W-III originally had an area of 5.66 acres which was later squared up by building an extension to the dike at the weir around the northeast corner, making the area 6.06 acres, or practically equal to W-IV. The first year of cultivation was for the purpose of building up the physical condition of the soil which was rather badly depleted. Therefore, in May 1941, soybeans were drilled parallel with the dividing dike on both watersheds (up and down the general slope) and then disked in, in September, and followed by a winter cover of rye. (See cropping procedures, fig. 20.) In May 1942, sweet corn was planted up and down the slope on W-III, but on four contour base lines on W-IV. In May 1943, baby lima beans were planted on both watersheds but the direction of tillage was interchanged. W-III was contour-planted following two base lines, and W-IV was planted up and down the slope, parallel with the dividing dike. (See pl. 7, p. 41.) Since runoffs during the row-crop season in 1943 were very light owing to subnormal rainfall, the same planting procedure was followed in 1944, using lima and edible soybeans. Winter cover of rye and vetch was planted in September both years. In September 1944, four cropland terraces were plowed in on W-III with a 2-bottom plow. Both W-III and W-IV were reduced to about 5 acres each and both planted on the contour in 1945. The soil profiles on both watersheds are deep and well-drained sandy loams and loams except that about 46 percent of W-IV runs to Beltsville loam and Hyattsville silt loam which have imperfect drainage. However, this is somewhat compensated for by a larger area of deposition (30 percent) of materials from higher slopes, compared with 10 percent on W-III. (See erosion map, fig. 19.)

The pastured watersheds W-VI and W-VII are about 3.5 acres each and lie on fairly steep irregular land that has eroded badly in the past. Runoffs from flat lands above are diverted to the woods on the east by diversion terraces, as shown in figure 21. The areas were seeded to pasture in 1939 and 1940 and a dike constructed between the areas in 1940. The pastures were gaged for 2.7 years under ordinary pasture management to get initial runoff characteristics. In May 1943, 14 contour furrows were plowed on W-VII, spaced 20 feet apart on the steepest slope. (See pl. 8, p. 42.) Vertical intervals between furrows ranged between 1.3 and 3.2 feet, with an average of 2.1 feet. It was estimated that the furrows would hold from 0.25 to 0.50 inch of runoff from the areas above them. Occasional cross-dams were placed in the furrows where they were slightly off-contour. W-VII is shallow and imperfectly drained, while W-VI is 46 percent imperfectly drained and 54 percent well-drained, and moderately deep.

Area W-VIII is a cut-over woodland of 2.43 acres on Beltsville silt loam which is imperfectly drained (fig. 22). The timber was logged off 15 to 25 years ago, and an understory of pine and hardwoods is coming in under the few unmerchantable trees which were left during the cutting. In places the growth is largely laurel and blueberries, with some spots bare of litter but moss-covered. The surface has been burned in the past, but probably not grazed. (See pl. 4, A, p. 22, for view of typical cover conditions.) The depth of precipitation is determined by a standard rain gage (S-6) located at the flume and intensities from other nearby recording gages.

W-IX is a mature woodland area of 12.05 acres, and had not been touched by an ax for many years by virtue of its inaccessible location far from roads and buildings. It runs largely to mixed hardwoods with some scrub pine. It has an excellent canopy overhead and continuous litter on the ground, and no evidence of burns. A typical view of woodland conditions is shown in plate 4, B. Precipitation is measured by R-5 located in a cleared area (isolated corn plot) 130 feet from the northeastern drainage line. Seventy-eight percent of the soils are moderately deep and well-drained. For maps of areas, see figure 22.

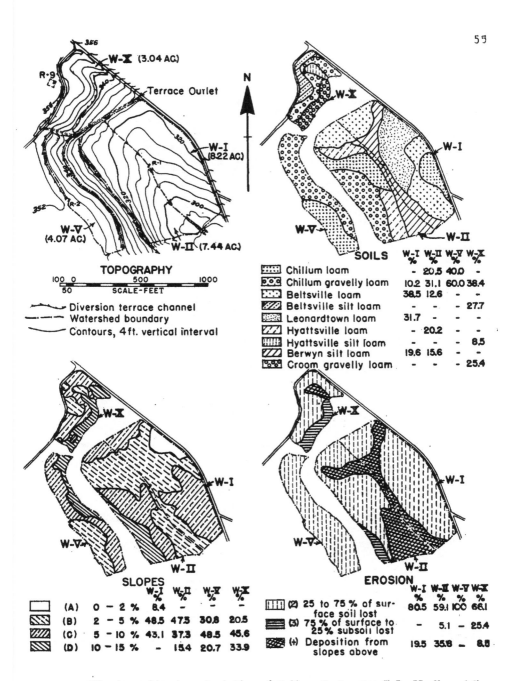

TOPOGRAPHY

| 100 | 0 | 500 | 1000 |
SCALE-FEET
50

～～～ Diversion terrace channel
—·—·— Watershed boundary
——— Contours, 4 ft. vertical interval

W-X (3.04 AC.)
R-9
Terrace Outlet
W-I (8.22 AC.)
W-V (4.07 AC.)
W-II (7.44 AC.)

N

SOILS

	W-I %	W-II %	W-V %	W-X %
Chillum loam	-	20.5	40.0	-
Chillum gravelly loam	10.2	31.1	60.0	38.4
Beltsville loam	38.5	12.6	-	-
Beltsville silt loam	-	-	-	27.7
Leonardtown loam	31.7	-	-	-
Hyattsville loam	-	20.2	-	-
Hyattsville silt loam	-	-	-	8.5
Berwyn silt loam	19.6	15.6	-	-
Croom gravelly loam	-	-	-	25.4

SLOPES

		W-I %	W-II %	W-V %	W-X %
☐	(A) 0 – 2 %	8.4	-	-	-
▨	(B) 2 – 5 %	48.5	47.5	30.8	20.5
▨	(C) 5 – 10 %	43.1	37.3	48.5	45.6
▨	(D) 10 – 15 %	-	15.4	20.7	33.9

EROSION

		W-I %	W-II %	W-V %	W-X %
▦	(2) 25 to 75 % of sur-face soil lost	80.5	59.1	100	66.1
▤	(3) 75 % of surface to 25 % subsoil lost	-	5.1	-	25.4
▨	(4) Deposition from slopes above	19.5	35.8	-	8.5

FIGURE 17. - Physiographic characteristics of College Park areas W-I, II, V, and X.

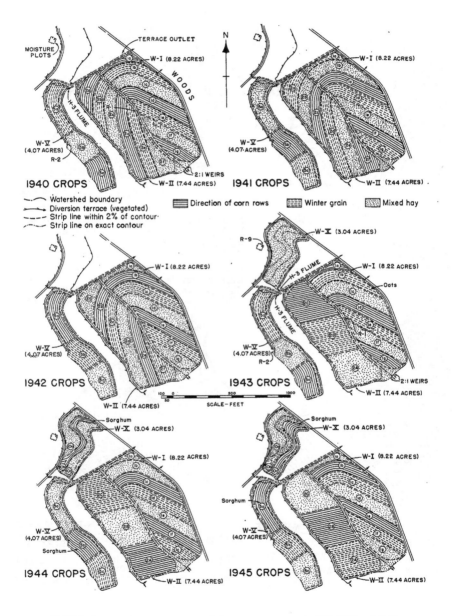

FIGURE 18.– Cropping procedures on College Park areas W-I, W-II, W-Ⅴ, and W-Ⅹ

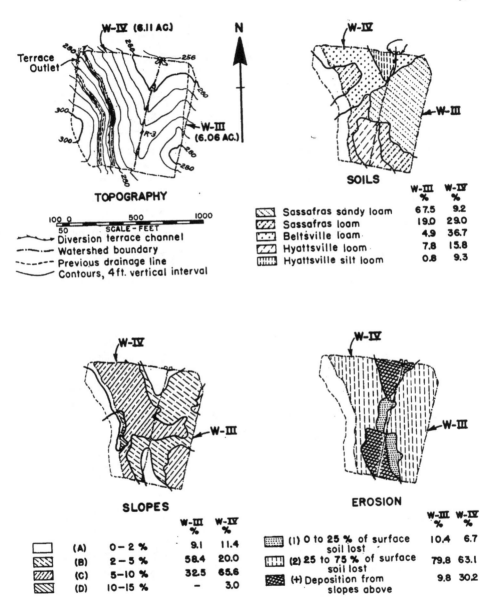

FIGURE 19.--Physiographic characteristics of College Park areas W-III and IV.

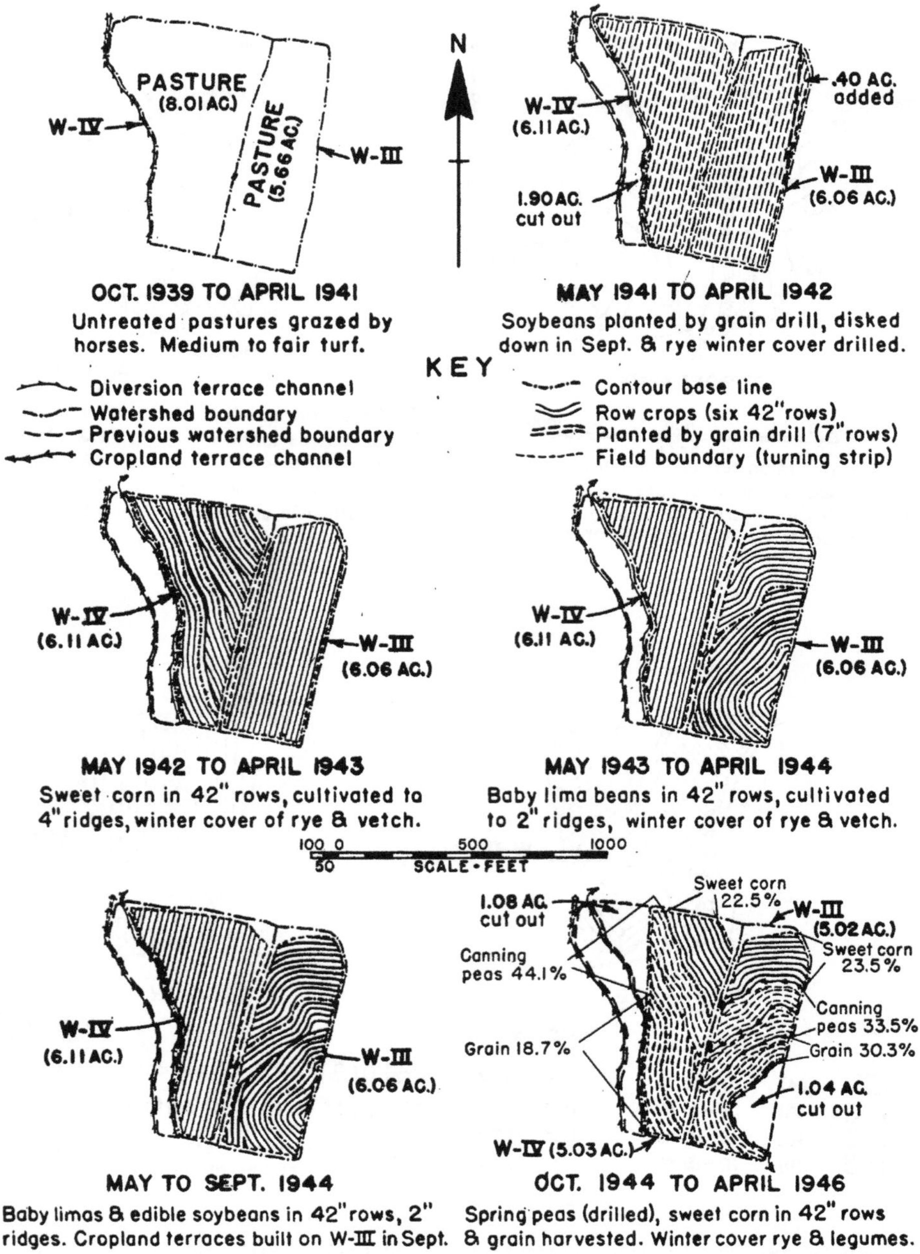
PASTURE (8.01 AC.)
PASTURE (5.66 AC.)
W-IV
W-III
N
OCT. 1939 TO APRIL 1941
Untreated pastures grazed by horses. Medium to fair turf.
W-IV (6.11 AC.)
.40 AC. added
1.90 AC. cut out
W-III (6.06 AC.)
MAY 1941 TO APRIL 1942
Soybeans planted by grain drill, disked down in Sept. & rye winter cover drilled.
KEY
Diversion terrace channel
Watershed boundary
Previous watershed boundary
Cropland terrace channel
Contour base line
Row crops (six 42" rows)
Planted by grain drill (7" rows)
Field boundary (turning strip)
W-IV (6.11 AC.)
W-III (6.06 AC.)
MAY 1942 TO APRIL 1943
Sweet corn in 42" rows, cultivated to 4" ridges, winter cover of rye & vetch.
W-IV (6.11 AC.)
W-III (6.06 AC.)
MAY 1943 TO APRIL 1944
Baby lima beans in 42" rows, cultivated to 2" ridges, winter cover of rye & vetch.
100 0 500 1000
50 SCALE-FEET
W-IV (6.11 AC.)
W-III (6.06 AC.)
MAY TO SEPT. 1944
Baby limas & edible soybeans in 42" rows, 2" ridges. Cropland terraces built on W-III in Sept.
1.08 AC. cut out
Sweet corn 22.5%
W-III (5.02 AC.)
Sweet corn 23.5%
Canning peas 44.1%
Canning peas 33.5%
Grain 18.7%
Grain 30.3%
1.04 AC. cut out
W-IV (5.03 AC.)
OCT. 1944 TO APRIL 1946
Spring peas (drilled), sweet corn in 42" rows & grain harvested. Winter cover rye & legumes.

FIGURE 20.--Cropping procedures for College Park areas W-III and IV.

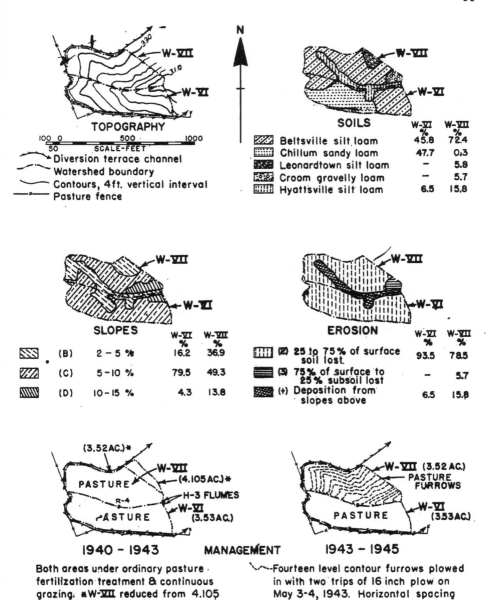

FIGURE 21.--Physiographic characteristics and pasture management on College Park areas W-VI and W-VII.

60

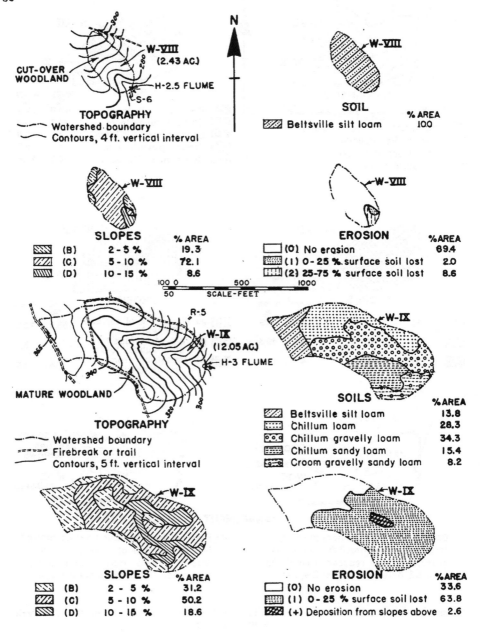

N

W-VIII
(2.43 AC.)

CUT-OVER
WOODLAND

H-2.5 FLUME

S-6

TOPOGRAPHY
Watershed boundary
Contours, 4 ft. vertical interval

W-VIII

SOIL
Beltsville silt loam

% AREA
100

W-VIII

SLOPES   % AREA
(B)   2 - 5 %   19.3
(C)   5 - 10 %   72.1
(D)   10 - 15 %   8.6

100 0   500   1000
50   SCALE-FEET

W-VIII

EROSION   % AREA
(0) No erosion   89.4
(1) 0 - 25 % surface soil lost   2.0
(2) 25-75 % surface soil lost   8.6

R-5

W-IX
(12.05 AC.)

H-3 FLUME

MATURE WOODLAND

TOPOGRAPHY
Watershed boundary
Firebreak or trail
Contours, 5 ft. vertical interval

W-IX

SOILS   % AREA
Beltsville silt loam   13.8
Chillum loam   28.3
Chillum gravelly loam   34.3
Chillum sandy loam   15.4
Croom gravelly sandy loam   8.2

W-IX

SLOPES   % AREA
(B)   2 - 5 %   31.2
(C)   5 - 10 %   50.2
(D)   10 - 15 % 18.6

W-IX

EROSION   % AREA
(0) No erosion   33.6
(1) 0 - 25 % surface soil lost   63.8
(+) Deposition from slopes above   2.6

FIGURE 22.--Physiographic characteristics and woodland management on College Park
areas W-VIII and IX.